Stock Market Investing for Beginners

The Top 101 Growth Stocks for 2019 – Including Marijuana Stocks, 5G Stocks, Penny Stocks and Dividends + How to Build a Starter Portfolio for Less than $100

Written By

Everyman Investing

Everyman Investing

© **Copyright 2019 - All rights reserved.**

The content contained within this book may not be reproduced, duplicated or transmitted without direct written permission from the author or the publisher.

Under no circumstances will any blame or legal responsibility be held against the publisher, or author, for any damages, reparation, or monetary loss due to the information contained within this book. Either directly or indirectly.

Legal Notice:

This book is copyright protected. This book is only for personal use. You cannot amend, distribute, sell, use, quote or paraphrase any part, or the content within this book, without the consent of the author or publisher.

Disclaimer Notice:

Please note the information contained within this document is for educational and entertainment purposes only. All effort has been executed to present accurate, up to date, and reliable, complete information. No warranties of any kind are declared or implied. Readers acknowledge that the author is not engaging in the rendering of legal, financial, medical or professional advice. The content within this book has been derived from various sources. Please consult a licensed professional before attempting any techniques outlined in this book.

By reading this document, the reader agrees that under no circumstances is the author responsible for any losses, direct or indirect, which are incurred as a result of the use of information contained within this document, including, but not limited to, — errors, omissions, or inaccuracies.

Table Of Contents

Introduction 5

Chapter One: Growth Stocks 7

Growth Industries 12

Chapter Two Value Stocks 33

How are Value Stocks Defined 33

Value Trading vs Growth Trading 35

Basics of Growth Investing 43

Chapter Three Growth Portfolio Allocations 48

Proper Allocation 52

Recession Proof Stocks 58

The Basic Investment Strategies 65

Chapter Four Growth Stocks Part 1 71

Chapter Five Growth Stocks Part 2 96

Chapter Six Growth Stocks Part 3 117

Chapter Seven Growth Stocks Part 4 136

Conclusion 155

Introduction

So you want to make a million dollars in the stock market? Is that possible and if it is, how does one accomplish it? Well, to answer both of those questions yes it is possible and there are many ways to accomplish it. For sure, it is easier if you have six figures to invest, but what if you only have five, four, or even three to get the job done? Yes, it can still be done with the right strategy and patience. It does not happen overnight and can take many years of up and down roller coaster riding to accomplish your goals. So you need to be prepared to choose the right stocks, leave your money in them, and watch the market religiously.

I am not talking about becoming a day trader watching a screen all day or someone chained to the stock market scroll, but just being someone that is aware of how trends affect companies and when to move or hold your position based on those. The best strategy is one where you do all of the research and leg work up front and then simply "lock and load" when it comes time to invest. That strategy is to pick the best growth stocks, invest early, and let your money grow with the stock. How do you pick those? By becoming aware of current business trends and growth industries from which the best growth stocks will come.

This book will give you the blueprint to choose from over 100 of them, starting for $100 or less. You will learn their industries, and be aware of how trends may change them in the future. The key to achieving financial freedom is to learn to spot those winners, invest, and hold. So, if you are ready to become a junior analyst and a wise investor, read on.

Chapter One: Growth Stocks

What are Growth Stocks? Well, in short, they are companies that grow higher than the market average. In addition, they do not give out dividends (or payments back to the stockholders for profits and growth each quarter) but instead, invest those back into the business to keep growing. When compared with traditional or Blue Chip stocks that pay those dividends, it can seem like a speculative or risky investment. However, what you must realize is that earnings from the rising stock price are usually more long term and outpace what might have come from a dividend. These stocks are usually tied to the hot growth industries which carry current biotech, marijuana, cloud technology, AI, 5G cellular, and nanotechnology. Their price on the exchange is considered their actual value no matter how high the price and you earn profits from the steady growth of the exchange price over a period of at least five years. Think of the appreciation of the price of a house or luxury car. It is much the same here, all profits are capital gains based on the resale of the stock. Very simple no muss no fuss and no complicated algorithms.

Here are some simple methods for picking Growth Stocks per Stockpicking.com

- Strong historical earnings growth. Companies should show a track record of strong earnings growth over the previous 5 to 10 years. The general idea is that if the company has displayed good growth in the recent past, it's likely to continue doing so moving forward.

- Strong forward earnings growth. Watch out for the release of the company's earnings reports (required by law for public corporations). This is an official public statement of a company's profitability for a specific period – typically a quarter or a year. These announcements are made on specific dates usually according to the quarter system and are linked to estimates that are issued by analysts. If it shows better than average or at least average growth, the stock is a good bet.

- Strong profit margins. A company's profit is calculated by deducting all expenses from sales (barring taxes) and dividing by sales. It's an important metric to consider because a company can have fantastic growth in sales but poor profit margins. This would mean that the upper management is not great at controlling costs in relation to revenues. If a company exceeds its previous five-year average of pretax profit margins – as well as those of its industry – the company may be a good growth candidate.

- Strong return on equity. The return on equity (ROE) measures its profit margin based on the money shareholders have invested. It's calculated by dividing net income by shareholder equity. Stable or increasing ROE indicates that management is doing a good job generating returns from shareholders' investments or money borrowed and is operating the business efficiently.

- Strong stock performance. In general, if a stock cannot realistically double in five years, **it's probably not a growth stock**. Keep in mind, a stock's price would double in seven years with a growth rate of just 10%. To double in five years, the growth rate must be 15%. But really it is much simpler, if you don't see growths of double, don't bother.

Ask a broker, a member of management, or yourself the following:

(Source: investopedia.com)

Question 1: *Where do you see sales trending in the next 12 to 24 months?*

A longer time period will give the investor a good glimpse of the opportunities and the risks that could present themselves over both the short and intermediate-term. Make sure you keep watch on the stock for an extended period.

Question 2: *What are the risks associated with the sourcing of raw material, or holding the line on costs of services?*

By asking this question, you will be able to learn whether there are any potential difficulties for the company in terms of acquiring raw materials or labor in the future. This can give you an idea of how the company's profit may change in the intermediate and long-term.

Question 3: *What is the best use for the cash on the company's balance sheet?*

This question will indicate whether the company is planning a large scale expansion or merger. It will also indicate whether or not they are a conservative type of management or are more interested in how they are perceived. Look for a response that would key in on whether the company is taking steps to improve its place in the market. If the company isn't growing and is losing cash, then you know what kind of performance to expect.

Question 4: *Who are the emerging competitors in the industry in which you operate?*

This question will let indicate whether they know who to watch out for and they're up against. It may also let you know of unknown rivals that may be coming to market, which could impact the company at some point down the road. Consequently, management may also disclose how it plans to deal with its new or existing competitors all together

Question 5: *What part or aspect of the business is giving*

you the most trouble now?

The answer will show weaknesses in the company's organization and provide some insight into future earnings. For example, if the manager indicates that one or more sections or divisions were unprofitable or too expensive to operate this will give you a good indication that there is a hole that needs to be plugged. Identifying problem areas is just one part of the equation. It is far more important to hear about solutions to the problem.

Question 6: *How close is Wall Street in terms of estimating your company's earnings results?*

With this question, you're asking if the company will meet or beat the street's estimate. If the manager indicates that they are always under or even overestimated by analysts then it could be an indication that the "street" is off on this company and that could be problematic.

Question 7: *What part of the business do you think is being ignored that has more upside potential than Wall Street is giving it?*

This question will show the managers passion. That could be an indicator that he/she or the entire management team has a positive outlook on the business. If they do not then that is a huge problem in itself. However, if they are overconfident in the face of contrary evidence, this could be a sign that they will run an unsubstantiated "maverick" strategy that in a solid company can be a huge advantage, but in a problem company can lead to ruin.

Question 8: *Do you have any plans to advance or promote the stock?*

Knowing whether management plans to promote the stock to all investors is a sign that either they believe in themselves or they don't. The savvy investor can buy into the stock ahead of what could be a large amount of buying pressure.

Question 9: *What catalysts will affect the stock going forward?*

The manager is likely to give the investor a wealth of information. This is due to the fact people like to talk about both their and their company's accomplishments. Whether or not they speak the facts will let you know what the future outlook will be. Including investment information about negative catalysts that could adversely impact the share price.

Growth Industries

No investment strategy suits every type of person all the time. This is particularly true for young Millennial and Generation Z investors. However, identifying growth stocks and industries is always a wise bet. As such, high-growth stocks are ideal for both young-adult and novice investors. Most young investors have 80% of their portfolio in stocks, and the remainder in safer, interest-yielding assets. Time is money and the extra time allows riskier investments to expand to their full potential. With the Bull Market we are experiencing, now is a perfect chance to take advantage of longer-term growth forecasts.

Whenever discussions about high-growth stocks arise, one must talk about e-commerce and how it overwhelmingly dominates the retail sector. Remember the newer generation has grown up in a time without the brick-and-mortar hegemony and thus is more inclined to participate in the e-commerce sector.

Considering that young people do nearly everything online, e-commerce companies that sell unorthodox items and charge a premium for them are the wave of the future. In addition, the fact that half of the US workforce will be independent contractors by 2020 also means that apps and companies intended to help with that transition will be a huge source of growth. For those of you who have worked in Fortune 500 or 100 companies, you have seen the intensity of big organizations. They need help to handle the needs of tens of thousands of workers and they need unified platforms to help find both employees and contractors.

Another factor is that by the time Millennials are looking at retirement, marijuana will have likely become legal. In fact, rumors are it may be legalized nationwide by 2020. Just as the Prohibition Era failed to curb Americans' desire for alcohol, the current period will fail to reduce people's desire for cannabis. This is in addition to the numerous beneficial uses of its derivatives. It's only a matter of time before the government listens to the will of the people. When that day comes, companies dealing in marijuana such as Cannabis Growth Corporation will exponentially rise in value.

Next, as more people are cashless and paying for things card-free with apps, any payment processor will be a great growth stock.

The world of virtual living and having everything in the home on a "smart system" is the next big thing. So, investing in companies that produce wireless and AI related products is a boon. Experts forecast that by the year 2020, home automation will become a $50 billion industry.

1. Biotech-In layman's terms is the process of combining biological elements with synthetic elements to produce a molecular change and a whole new product or function from the originals. This is what the companies that make up this sector do. The sector is divided into four different categories of companies. Those that make products for healthcare, agriculture/food, industrial (chemicals for cleaning and non-edible function including environmentally friendly products), fuel, land preservation, and warfare. The Biotech Industry is divided into many different subcategories based on the sub-

sector they serve:

A. Gold Biotech - these are companies that use computer components and mechanics to affect biological issues-such as pharma and medical technologies for surgery or treatment.

B. Blue Biotech - this centers on the use of sea algae to create new sources of fuel.

C. Green Biotech - these companies focus on agriculture and genetic manipulation of seeds and waste/pest reduction.

D. Red Biotech - companies focusing on genetic engineering for disease prevention like stem cells.

E. White Biotech - focuses on new chemicals or enzymes that can make the manufacturing process cheaper and faster.

F. Yellow Biotech - focuses on food production and new genetic strains of food crops.

G. Gray Biotech - focuses on the preservation of ecological diversity and lowering levels of pollution.

H. Brown Biotech - these companies focus on rehabilitating arid areas like desserts to make them capable of supporting life.

Everyman Investing

    I. Violet Biotech - focuses on using technology to solve social issues.

    J. Dark Biotech - focuses on the darker side of Biotech such as chemical and biological weapons.

2.Marijuana - Companies that make up the thriving and new cannabis industry comprise this grouping. They don't just cover the growth, harvest, production, and sale of the actual plant, but also things like cannabis oil products and various ingestion tools (bongs, pipes, and e-cigs). In addition, things made from byproducts of the plant like hemp fabric, fuel (can cross over into biotech), and hemp protein food products. Cannabis was first legalized in Uruguay in 2013 and Canada in 2018, with many other countries discussing it. As for the USA, the states vary (as shown in the below chart from Map of Marijuana).

State	Legal Status	Medicinal	Decriminalized
Alabama	Fully Illegal	No	No
Alaska	Fully Legal	Yes	Yes

Arizona	Mixed	Yes	No
Arkansas	Mixed	Yes	No
California	Fully Legal	Yes	Yes
Colorado	Fully Legal	Yes	Yes
Connecticut	Mixed	Yes	Reduced
Delaware	Mixed	Yes	Reduced
District of Columbia	Fully Legal	Yes	Yes
Florida	Mixed	Yes	No
Georgia	Mixed	Yes	No
Hawaii	Mixed	Yes	No
Idaho	Fully Illegal	No	No

Illinois	Mixed	Yes	Reduced
Indiana	Fully Illegal	No	No
Iowa	Fully Illegal	No	No
Kansas	Fully Illegal	No	No
Kentucky	Fully Illegal	No	No
Louisiana	Mixed	Yes	No
Maine	Fully Legal	Yes	Yes
Maryland	Mixed	Yes	Reduced
Massachusetts	Fully Legal	Yes	Yes
Michigan	Fully Legal	Yes	Yes
Minnesota	Mixed	Yes	Reduced

Mississippi	Fully Illegal	No	Reduced
Missouri	Mixed	Yes	Reduced
Montana	Mixed	Yes	No
Nebraska	Fully Illegal	No	Reduced
Nevada	Fully Legal	Yes	Yes
New Hampshire	Mixed	Yes	Reduced
New Jersey	Mixed	Yes	No
New Mexico	Mixed	Yes	Reduced
New York	Mixed	Yes	Reduced
North Carolina	Fully Illegal	No	Reduced

North Dakota	Mixed	Yes	No
Ohio	Mixed	Yes	Reduced
Oklahoma	Mixed	Yes	No
Oregon	Fully Legal	Yes	Yes
Pennsylvania	Mixed	Yes	No
Rhode Island	Mixed	Yes	Reduced
South Carolina	Fully Illegal	No	No
South Dakota	Fully Illegal	No	No
Tennessee	Fully Illegal	No	No
Texas	Fully Illegal	No	No
Utah	Mixed	Yes	No

Vermont	Fully Legal	Yes	Yes
Virginia	Fully Illegal	No	No
Washington	Fully Legal	Yes	Yes
West Virginia	Mixed	Yes	No
Wisconsin	Fully Illegal	No	No
Wyoming	Fully Illegal	No	No

As you may guess this is still rather volatile as it is not fully legal in the USA and has only just started on the international front, but the outlook is bright with news that North American sales of cannabis and related products topped 6.7 billion in 2016. Colorado and California alone generated 226 million and 345 million, respectively, in additional taxes during the tax year 2018. These numbers have been increasing by a rate of 30% every year in both sales and taxes. It is evident that both the private and public sector already see the potential to generate money with marijuana and that full legalization is on the distant horizon.

Everyman Investing

In addition, the sale of non-Tetrahydrocannabinol (THC-the enzyme that produces the high in marijuana) marijuana is readily available in all 50 states and in many countries in which the full substance is still illegal. Revenue from the sale of these products is expected to hit 22 billion by 2022. Edibles and oils made with Cannabis oil have been cited as an essential oil and are considered very beneficial in treating things like:

1. Anxiety/depression-initial tests in animals and humans show that applying the oil can calm panic attacks and help prevent them.

2. Pain-the anti-inflammatory properties of the oil have been shown to help reduce chronic pain by up to 15% in humans.

3. Heart Health-initial testing reveals that the application of a few drops has been able to reduce the inflammation that can contribute to cardiovascular events.

4. Nausea-it has been shown that the oil can help reduce feelings of uneasiness and nausea by 9%.

5. Skin Ailments-the oil is undergoing studies that show it may help reduce skin irritation and clear acne.

6. Antipsychotic Effects-studies suggest that CBD may help people by reducing psychotic symptoms.

7. Substance Abuse Treatment-CBD has been shown to modify circuits in the brain related to drug addiction and reduce substance dependence.

8. Anti-tumor Effects-in test-tube and animal studies CBD has demonstrated that it can slow the spread of breast, prostate, brain, colon and lung cancer.

9. Diabetes Prevention-in mice it reduced the incidence/symptoms of diabetes by 56%.

Source Healthline.com

The uses of the related Cannabis Plant Protein called Hemp are also a source of great economic and societal boons as we are discovering more and more about it. Sales of Hemp products are estimated to be at 2.6 Billion by 2022 and cover a variety of markets and uses like:

1. Pet Food-the protein has shown great promise in the production of animal feed by using the heavy and easily digestible protein in pet food, especially for those with sensitive stomachs.

2. Human Food-the protein can make a variety of things for human consumption as it is full of amino acids. Vegan and vegetarian products like powders and faux meats are already made of hemp and things like salad dressings, cooking oils, and flour can be made from the seeds.

3. Fabric-hemp has been shown to be capable of being made into sturdy fabrics to produce clothes/bedding/industrial materials.

4. Oil Bases-hemp seed oil can be reduced to a pure oil to serve as a lubricant for industrial use and as a base for consumer products like lotions.

5. Fuel-the fuel industry has long been doing research on the use of hemp as a fossil fuel alternative. Currently, it's being used in biodiesel and ethanol.

6. Paper-paper made from hemp is of high quality and the production of hemp is much easier and take up less space than other paper/food producing plants.

7. Concrete-hemp particles can provide the base for a form of cement that is just as strong as other types. It is currently being used in home construction.

Source: cannabis reports

The sale of Marijuana-Related accessories and products has already topped 20 million per year in the USA alone, so it is also a booming market. The breakdown of products is shown below from Marijuana Business Daily.

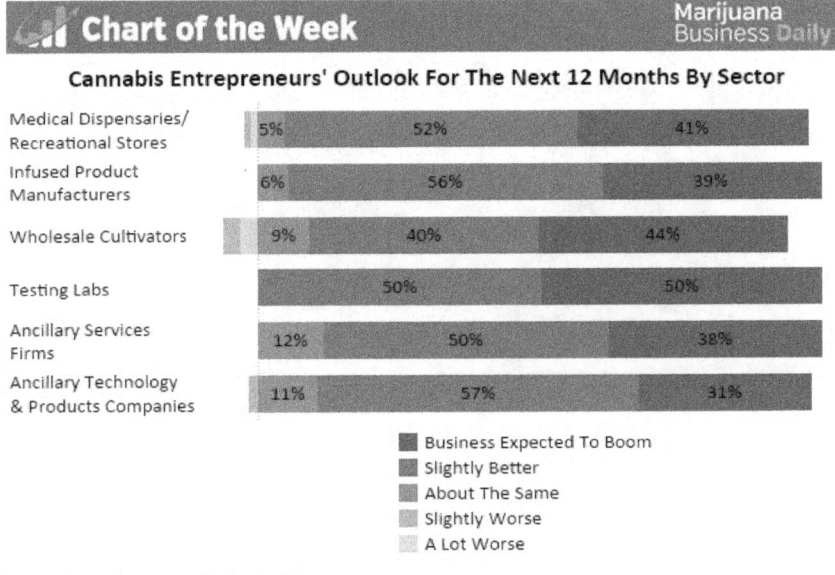

3. Cloud Technology-the process and tools that allow for transfer and storage of information. Anything that stores or allows you to pull/transmit/share information (including e-commerce) from the web is included in this category. The big boys like Apple, Microsoft, Amazon, and Google are part of this sector. The types of products in this sector include software, hardware, and online offerings, as demonstrated by the below graphic from computing.com.

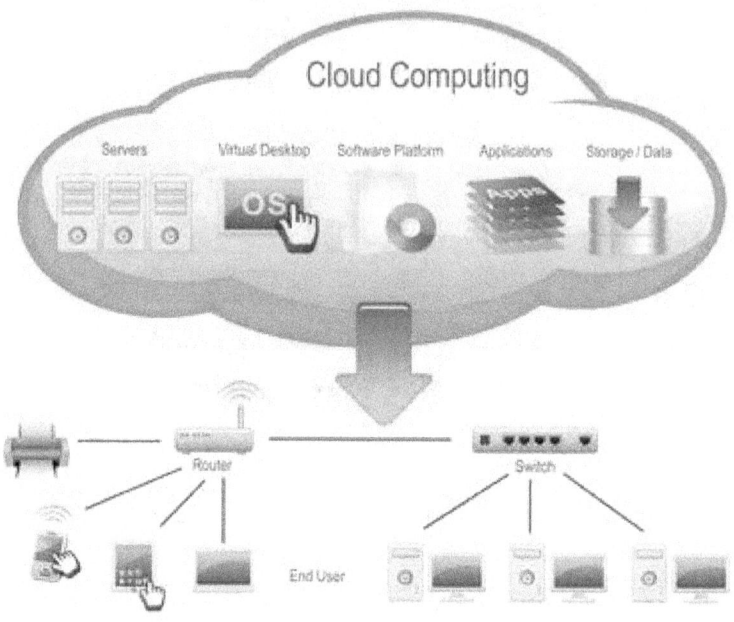

No matter what age or technological level you are at you use cloud computing, and this list will give you some idea of how far-reaching it is. The use of cloud technology is becoming the norm and is no longer an extra feature. Costly and bulky options like disc related software and storage have virtually been eliminated in favor of more efficient and less space restrictive options. Sales of cloud technology made up 85% of total IT sales in 2017 and represent a 200 billion dollar industry. Cloud computing services provide users with a series of functions including:

- Email

- Storage, backup, and data retrieval

- Creating and testing apps

- Analyzing data

- Audio and video streaming

- Delivering software on demand

Source: Azure.com

4. Artificial Intelligence (AI)-This sector revolves around products and technology that use mimicking of the human brain/personality to operate. Think Alexa, Bigsby, or Google Assistant, though there is so much more involved in this sector and new companies are emerging every day with new systems that mimic human interaction. These technologies are breaking into industries like transportation, software, e-commerce, and security. Sales and development of AI topped 108 Billion in 2018 and AI is one of the fastest growing sectors in the world. Predictions state that the following AI based industries as going to grow by at least 50% in the next 50 years:

1. Accounting-taxes and basic bookkeeping will be done by software. I mean think about it, when was the last time you went to a physical tax preparer?

2. Finance/Brokerage-most if not all investing will be done online, the onset of technology has virtually eliminated the middle person or broker.

3. Banking-online banks have exploded and teller-less

banks are already becoming the norm with over 80% of deposits and transactions are done using ATMs, on Apps, or online.

4. Pharmaceuticals-using AI to tabulate the data side of research will become the norm, as well as robotic solutions in compounding elements in the lab.

5. Design-AI will soon do the majority of design tabulations for certain industries by generating precise models for blueprints and sketches.

6. Government Planning-AI will become the basis for things like smart cities and we may even become able to vote online.

7. Telecommunications-automated bill payment, payment arrangements, and even changing your plan is already becoming the norm. When was the last time you paid the extra fee to speak with a person?

8. Purchasing-AI will soon make it possible to do automatic reordering of supplies or even to predict what is needed for a particular time span. This is already used in the restaurant industry with interactive Point of Sale, but it is being adapted for other industries as well.

9. Insurance/investments-purchasing of insurance online is already the standard, as well as making payments

and making changes via many apps. In fact, new technologies allow rates to be set by tracking your actual driving behavior rather than age groups.

10. Medical Records-digital medical records have been the standard since 2005.

11. Health Care-new AI will allow surgeons to do more complex procedures by mapping down to the nano-cell and are even capable of doing some procedures on their own.

12. Transportation-self driving cars and trucks are being tested and will hit the roads within 50 years. Tesla and Uber are already testing autonomous vehicles in several cities.

See some examples below from AI.com.

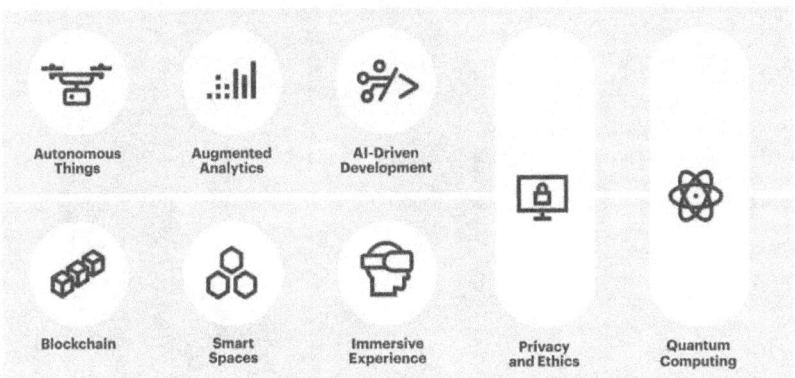

5. 5G Cellular and Wireless-5G stands for the 5th generation of wireless technology and holds promises of speeds 100 times faster than 4G and 10 times faster than the best broadband. In the next 50 years, we will see this technology lead to autonomous vehicles, smart cities, smart factories, and much more. The download, upload, and data transfer to all devices will be seamless and further merge the global economy into a more cohesive unit. Revenue from the development and sale of 5G already tops 15.7 billion and growing. Not everyone has made the jump to 5G, but all will eventually come on board with major players like Verizon, AT&T, Sprint, China Mobile, Cisco, and Google leading the pack. The estimates are 326 billion dollars in capital will be needed to establish 5g by 2025 and to be a part of most industries by 2026. These companies will continue to experience growth and investors will be rewarded.

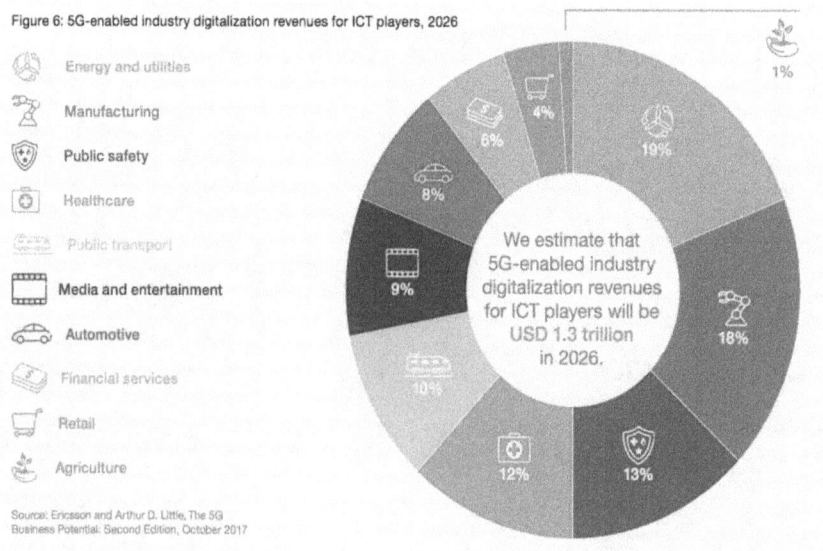

Figure 6: 5G-enabled industry digitalization revenues for ICT players, 2026

Source: Ericsson and Arthur D. Little, The 5G Business Potential, Second Edition, October 2017

6. Nanotechnology-is a sector dealing with the manipulation and research of extremely small particles of 100 nanometers or less. These particles will lead to greater energy output with less strain on resources. The possibilities for the use of nano-energy in green technologies are endless and represent the hope of what will become the future technological standard as we must reduce dependence on fossil fuels and other energy sources that take up a great deal of resources or space. Also, the ability to manipulate cellular components will propel research into genetic conditions and diseases like cancer in the future, as we can possibly cure or prevent them with the use of nanotechnology. In addition, the manipulation of microparticles of many different elements has a wide variety of consumer and personal uses as shown below.

1. **Medicine-**Nanotechnology is already being used in medicine to deliver nanoparticles that contain drugs or other substances, or that target heat or light to microorganisms and diseased cells such as cancer cells. As well as the manipulation of stem cells and other genetic material to treat and prevent disease.

2. **Electronics-**Nano electronics have already developed space saving capabilities as their weight and power consumption are significantly less than traditional electronics.

3. **Environment-**Nanotechnology has many

applications aimed at improving the environment such as cleaning up polluted areas through the use of waste eating microbes or improving manufacturing methods to prevent unnecessary waste.

4. **Consumer Products-**Nanotechnology has already found its way into numerous consumer products such as skin care with micro delivery of vitamins and making fabrics flame resistant by coating fibers.

Source: cceweek.com

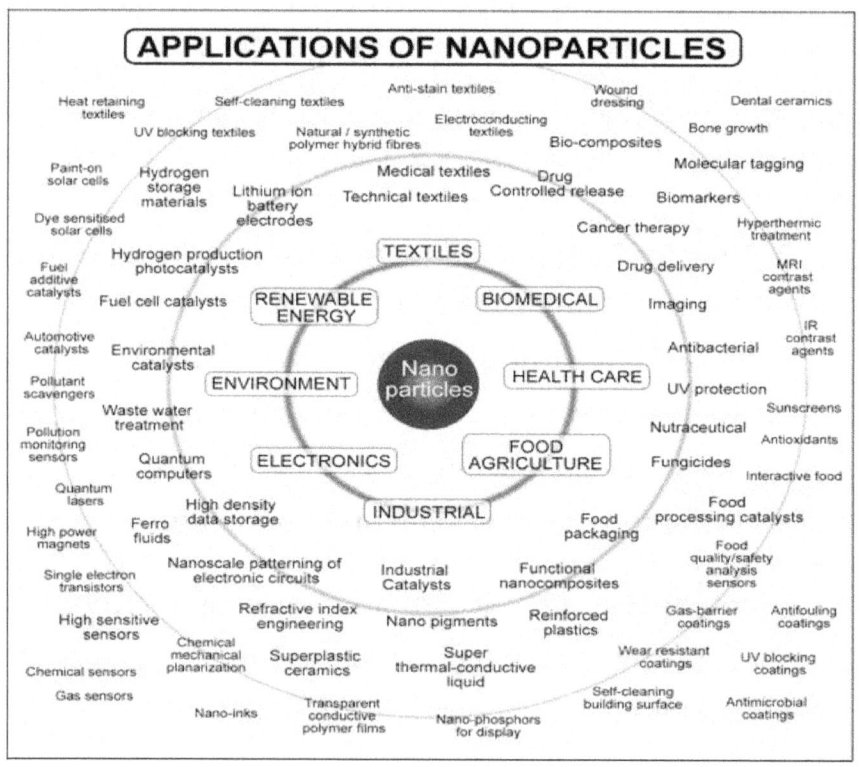

Chapter Two Value Stocks

How are Value Stocks Defined

Value stocks are stocks that have solid fundamentals and are priced well below their competitors in their respective fields. The determination of the "value of the stock" is based on the opinions of Wall Street Analysts, Brokers, and Peers in the same industry. As you can probably guess, this is highly speculative and not an exact science. The primary thing to remember is that value stocks are not always growth stocks. The stock is measured on its intrinsic value or true value based on factors such as its profits, P & L, stability, and potential for future growth. These are determined by many different methods and will vary by a few dollars analyst to analyst. Most of these companies will offer dividends or shares of their profits in good quarters to investors which is another source of profit and an enticement to choose the company's stock. This type of trading (with the exception of dividends) is true for not only stocks but bonds and commodities such as sugar and coffee on their own markets. These are stocks that provide income in ways other than just capital gains from sale or stock price. Though that appreciation is present, holders of value stock are more concerned with getting cash for dividends and bonuses.

Here are a few questions to ask a broker about value stocks:

Everyman Investing

- What is the status of your fund and how is it structured, do you specialize in value vs growth stocks?

- Do you have a specific industry or geographic focus for your investments and how much value is expected for value stocks?

- What are your most successful investments and what is their payout history?

- What metrics are you tracking when considering an investment in a value stock and do you keep accurate records of the payouts?

- How many investments do you make per year, and what is your typical investment size?

If you are interested, here is a list of the top value stocks of the current year

1. Eaton (ETN, $69.11) which is priced at less than 15 times trailing profits and roughly 12 times next year's projected earnings.

2. FedEx (FDX, $173.96) is still a solid business, but its growth is limited in the delivery industry.

3. Allstate (ALL, $86.49) lost almost a quarter of its value between late September and Christmas, prompted in large part by Hurricane Florence battering the East

Coast and Hurricane Michael hitting the Gulf Coast.

4. AT&T (T, $30.67) is down roughly 30% from its 2016 peak, reaching fresh multi-year lows in December before bouncing back to still-depressed levels.

5. Pentair (PNR, $40.54) shares broadly continued the downward trek they began shortly before the recent spinoff was even announced.

6. Electronic Arts (EA, $90.47) is down nearly 40% of their value since their peak in 2018.

7. Caterpillar (CAT, $124.37) – Many experts say that the new tariffs and other trade regulations will cause this market price to drop, but that the dividends and other perks will make this a key value stock

8. Bank of America (BAC, $29.63) has dipped below $23 twice in the last year, but the fact that its day to day operations remain strong makes this great for income, but not growth.

9. AbbVie (ABBV, $77.14) has had a rough 2018 but overall have had some peaks and valleys that raised the price to back above $38 per share.

Value Trading vs Growth Trading

The strategy of value investing/trading was created in the 1930s by David Dodd and Ben Graham (Ivy League Finance

Everyman Investing

Professors) with the publishing of their book, "Security Analysis" which has become the standard for all analysis. Until the 21st century, most traditional investing was based on value investing and relied on "reading charts" to guess what the future value of a stock would be. The intrinsic value (guessed value) minus the market price is the margin of safety and most investors would practice the risky technique of betting the stock will stay in the safety zone to make money. If you buy at the value price and then it climbs to the intrinsic price on the market then you win, if it falls below the purchase price you lose.

To protect themselves some value investors use an even more complicated hedge system of "puts" and "calls" to protect themselves in value investing. This is done on a secondary market that bundles the calls or puts them into another type of security. It consists of buying a call option on the stock or the right to buy at a low price (to protect themselves from buying high) or a put option that permits them to sell at a certain price (to protect from selling low). So, to have this type of insurance one must buy the stock, then purchase a call or put on a secondary market to "hedge" their bet on the stock. If the designated price or strike price is reached then the investor can use the hedge and someone will sell to them or buy from them at the strike price. The investor who owns the stock has the right to any gains on the stock price and any dividends, while those on the secondary market of puts and calls do not.

Wow, that all sounds complicated and it is. That is why I highly recommended the simpler method of buying growth stocks and making your profits from the rise in the price. The use of Hedge and Value Investing gave rise to the behemoth of Wall Street that you see in movies about the 1980s. This was where investment banks and brokers made their money and in many ways caused the recession of 2007. They took the model of the secondary "put and call" options and expanded it to selling things like mortgages as securities. This created a huge "middle person" giant of those that took the orders from clients and executed the trades or secondary trades.

Options may seem overwhelming, but they're actually very easy to understand if you know how to look at them. As you learn more, you may realize this is not the type of investing you are interested in, but I feel a thorough understanding of both types is needed to grow as an investor. Yes, you are starting as a simple growth investor, but as your money and expertise grow so will your interest in other types of investments. Most complex or mixed portfolios are usually constructed with several asset classes. These may be stocks, bonds, ETFs, mutual funds, preferred stocks, and alternative investments. Options are just another asset class, and when used properly, they offer many advantages to other types of investing.

They are powerful because they enhance a portfolio with added income, protection, and leverage. There is usually an option that is appropriate for any investor's goal. Often (as previously mentioned) they are used as a guard or hedge against a declining stock market or instrument to limit losses. They can also be used to produce monthly or quarterly income.

As with other types of investments, there is no guarantee with options. Trading them involves certain risks that the investor must be aware of before making a trade. In fact, you often see them sold with this or other types of disclaimers.

"Options involve risks and are not suitable for everyone. Options trading can be speculative in nature and carry substantial risk of loss." (Source Investopedia)

Most options belong to securities known as derivatives, which are often associated with risk-taking and massive speculations. Think the speculation on home mortgages prior to 2008, they were a form of derivative. However, the overall bad perception of derivatives is really overblown. Derivative means that its price is dependent on the price of something else. Options are derivatives of other types of stocks and investments and are therefore dependent on them. On the overall standard, a stock option typically represents 100 shares of the stock.

If you buy or sell an option contract it grants you the right to buy or sell the contract but does not require you to move on the underlying asset at a set price on or before a certain date. Call options give the holder the right to buy a stock (as bundles in an option) and a put gives the holder the right to sell a stock (as bundled in the option).

To demonstrate the two types of options look at the following:

For a call option, an investor gets wind of a potential extra offering of a marijuana stock. The investor decided he or she wants the right to purchase that stock in the future, depending on certain parameters that are advantageous to the investor. These circumstances would affect their decision to buy the stock, think the USA legalizing marijuana at a future date. The investor would benefit from the option of buying or not. They can buy a call option on the stock which gives them the ability to buy the stock at $10.00 per share at any point in the next three years. They secure the purchase with a nonrefundable deposit to secure the option to call (think call for the sale).

The cost or payment is the premium for the option. It is the price of the option contract. The deposit might be $30,000 that the buyer pays for the stock. Let's say three years have passed, and the USA has legalized weed and its sub-products. The investor exercises the option and buys the stock for $10 per share, even though the price has rocketed to #20 per share. However, if legalization does not happen, the investor must still buy the stock at 10 per share, even if the price is hovering around 8 to 11 per share. That is the contract. The 30k premium is still kept as that was the price for the right to buy.

Now, as to a put option, if you own the Marijuana Stock a put option would be an insurance policy on the value of the stock in the future. The investor may fear that a bear (down) market is near and may be unwilling to lose more than 10% of their position in the stock. If the stock is currently trading at $10 per share, they can buy a put option giving the right to sell the index at 9.90 per share, at any point in the designated time period.

If the price falls to 7 in the next few years they limited their losses to 10% or pennies on the share and if the stock goes up, they are under no obligation to sell at 9.90 per share. Therefore they only lose the premium paid, unless they can later sell at a higher price.

Buying a stock instantly gives you a long position while buying a call option gives you a possible long position in the stock. If you sell a naked or uncovered call, this gives you a possible short position in the underlying stock. However, buying a put option gives you a possible short position on the stock. Selling a naked position in a put gives you a possible long position in the stock. Keeping these four possibilities straight in your head is crucial.

Finally, to understand options here are some general terms you must know.

The seller of an option is called its writer

The strike price of an option contract is the agreed price the stock in question is bought or sold.

When an option is in-the-money it means the buyer came out on the positive end of the contract.

The expiration date is the precise date that the option contract terminates.

Options can be traded on a national options exchange, such as the Chicago Board Options Exchange or CBOE, those are called listed options.

These types of options have fixed strike prices and expiration dates and each contract represents 100 shares of a stock.

The amount which an option is in-the-money is its intrinsic value.

When an option is out-of-the-money the option for the buyer is on the negative end of the purchase or sell.

The total cost or price of an option is the premium and is dependent on:

   1. Stock price

2. Strike price

3. Time remaining until expiration (time value)

4. Volatility or history of the movement of the stock

Speculation is a wager or bet on the future price direction of a stock and of the derivative that the option is based on.

Hedging with options is meant to reduce risk at a reasonable cost, think of an insurance policy for stocks, this is an option.

Spreads are the difference between the strike price and purchase price.

Combinations are trades constructed with both a call and a put.

An option is the potential to participate in a future price change. So, if you own a call, you can participate in the upward movement of a stock without owning the stock. You have the option to participate or not to participate, based on your best interests.

For many of us, a middle-man is necessary in a value-based system because of the expertise required to make money. This type of expertise is something most of us do not have and we fare better in a simpler system. The secondary market has largely gone away on Wall Street with the advent of new technologies that allow the common person to trade from a computer or smartphone directly with the market, without a middle person.

Though some middle experts are needed for larger transactions, for most of us the simplicity of trading today is adequate. This new simple method is known as the Growth Market and is what we will concentrate on. Also within the realm of Value Trading is the market (Pink Sheets) that involve very small companies known as "Penny Stocks", they are companies with very cheap prices that the investor feels are poised to grow exponentially.

Bigger companies can have inflated prices since everyone's paying attention to them, while small-cap stocks tend to have fewer people that even know about them. Less risky investors stay away from them since they tend to be risky and most group investors (mutual funds) have restrictions when it comes to investing in them. They are more volatile and therefore difficult to trade.

Basics of Growth Investing

Remember you only need to be right once or twice (1000%+ returns) to secure financial freedom for the rest of your life and we will be looking at the stocks and stock strategy that can make that happen. In contrast to value investors, growth investors buy stock in companies that may be trading for more than their intrinsic or estimated value. They make decisions based on the same charts, but with the added element of market trends and past market performance. The growth investor assumes that the price or value (no matter what it is) will grow over the long term and bring them profit with the spread between the purchase price and future value. This is why people buy 500 shares of Apple or Google at 200 plus dollars a share because they see the potential for a modest profit in the future. If you choose correctly over a volume of trades that modest profit turns into a huge profit. Ultimately, growth investors seek to increase their profit through capital appreciation, much like those that flip houses or cars. The profit is in the resale price.

Growth investors seek to invest in companies whose earnings are expected to grow at a faster rate than the rest of the market average or the average of their own sectors. So they tend to focus on younger/newer companies or proven companies with growth potential. Their theory is that positive performance by the company in their actual operations will equate to better market performance and higher returns on the price of their stock. Most of these companies (as we pointed out in chapter one) are in the growth or hot industries that are developing the technologies, services, and products that will become popular or essentials in the future. The focus is entirely on growth in the stock price not on the payout of investor dividends since most of these growing companies reinvest their earnings rather than paying investors or executives.

Predicting the hot growth companies is not an exact science

and it requires some case by case interpretation and judgment. No matter what method you utilize it takes a degree of both gambling instinct and hard past performance data. Investors use certain criteria as a framework for their analysis, but these methods must be applied with the company's individual situation in mind. No two companies are alike even if they operate in the same sector or develop competing products. For example, Apple and Samsung both dominate smartphone sales but are very different companies and offer products for very different types of consumers. They must each be considered on their own, apart from each other or other producers of smartphones or wireless products.

Growth stocks trade on any exchange and in any sector, but you'll usually find them in the current growth industries (which we highlighted in chapter one). However, there are some average guidelines you might use to point out yet unrecognized growth companies to invest in.

- Strong historical earnings growth. Companies should show a track record of strong earnings growth over the previous five to 10 years. The minimum EPS growth depends on the size of the company, but returns or growth that averages 3% to 10% is a good gauge. Why this range? 3% to 5% is average growth for most businesses, so choosing ones with at least that much is a good indicator of success and of course over that is just gravy. The basic idea is that if the company has displayed average to good growth in the last 5 to 10 years, it's likely to continue doing so over the next 5 to 10 years.

- Strong Earnings Reports from the company itself is a huge indicator. An earnings report is a release that outlines the company's profitability for a specific period usually for the most recently elapsed quarter or year. It's these estimates that garner a lot of attention from investors, as they are usually a great indicator of how the company will do measured against the others in the sector.

- Strong profit margins. A company's profits are calculated by deducting all expenses from sales (except taxes) and dividing by sales. It's an important metric to consider because a company can have fantastic growth in sales with poor gains in earnings. Basically, a company can show 1 billion in gross revenues, but once everything is deducted (save taxes) they may only show 10 million in earnings (taxable). This could indicate that management is not controlling costs and is allowing revenue to be eaten up by expenses. No company will survive if this ratio is off and so a company that exceeds its previous average of pretax profit margins and those of its sector could be a good growth candidate.

- Strong return on equity (ROE). This measures how much profit a company produces when compared with the money shareholders invest. It's calculated by dividing net income (revenues after taxes and expenses have been deducted) by shareholder equity (dollar amount held in shares by investors). Compare a company's present ROE to the five-year average ROE of the company and the industry. If the number is stable or increasing, then the ROE indicates that management is doing a good job protecting investor money and giving them a return on their investment (ROI).

- Strong stock performance. This is the simplest method because, in general, if a stock cannot realistically double its returns over a 10 year period than it is not a growth stock. To double in 10 years, a company's growth must be at least 7% to 10% per year for every year in the period. Some industries returns might average at a 50% growth, which only requires a 5% return year over year, so take it case by case.

Source: Bush Investments

Chapter Three Growth Portfolio Allocations

When investing, particularly for long-term goals, there are two things you will likely hear about frequently, Allocation and Diversification. Diversification helps buffer or limit an investors risk or exposure to loss in any one type of investment or one type of industry. Allocation or the range or mix of your investments will provide the guide or outline for your choices of investments. Truly understanding how the two work can help you comprise or build a portfolio that really meets your needs and goals, while only incurring your desired level of risk.

Generally, diversification deals with the process of investing in a number of different instruments to help negate risk. The basic idea is that if some of your investments in your portfolio lose or decline in value that others may increase or hold fast. For example, say you wanted to invest in mostly single or basic stocks, there is a way to diversify even in a single asset class (a type of investment). Rather than investing in just the stocks of American companies or companies based wherever you are in the world, you could mix up your portfolio or asset mix by investing in the stocks of companies in foreign nations, as well. Also, instead of just relying on "Blue Chip", large caps, or the stocks of well-known or older companies (think IBM, Google/Alphabet, Kraft Foods), you could mix it up by investing in startups or smaller/less well-known companies (small caps or medium caps).

For those of you that prefer the more stable instruments like bonds for income, you could choose a mix or both government and corporate bonds to potentially take advantage the higher returns on corporate bonds, while negating the risk with the more stable government issue bonds. Also, instead of relying on one type of maturity within bonds, you could mix it up on the maturity dates, with a mix of 5, 10, 20-year bonds, or even longer. Remember that longer-term bonds tend to react more dramatically to interest rate functions than shorter-term bonds. So, interest rates will have less effect on a five-year bond than a 20-year bond.

For those that wish to venture outside things like stocks and bonds, there is the world of currency trading on the FOREX. This is basically buying blocks of a foreign currency and then selling when its value increases. This requires a little more day trading and daily watching of the news and political events to grasp, but it is a great way to generate short term (less than 5 year) gains.

Asset allocation is a strategic way to align your portfolio with different asset classes that will maximize your returns while severely limiting your risk in a downturn. After researching all your investment goals, timeline, and fear or tolerance to risk. Then you would then invest different amounts of money (for a different percentage) of your portfolio in a range of different instruments to reach your goals while keeping your risk of loss down at a level you are willing to accept. A careful study and grasp of these three factors will guide your choices and help you make the right decisions.

Overall, a large profit margin or accumulation level, a high-risk tolerance, and a long timeline will usually translate into a more aggressive portfolio or a strategy with a higher concentration in more risky instrument types. This will naturally lead to more money or a higher percentage of your portfolio invested in long term growth investments. A common example of an aggressive or growth strategy is 70% stocks, 20% bonds, and 10% cash. On the flip side, a person whose goal is a shorter timeline, with less risk in exchange for more moderate gains would require a more conservative approach. Such a conservative or income-oriented strategy would be 50% bonds, 30% stocks and real estate, and 20% cash.

Just remember that over time, a portfolio's allocations can shift due to changing market performance. In bull (up) market years when the stock market performs particularly well, a portfolio may become heavy in stocks, while in years when bonds outperform, they may end up comprising a larger percentage of a portfolio. So, for the investor who wished to follow a formula, a little bit of rebalancing may be in order to compensate for the change in the market.

There are generally two ways to rebalance a portfolio. The first is by simply selling any over-weighted asset classes (instruments) and directing the proceeds into the under-weighted assets. The second is to direct new investments (assets) into the under-weighted asset class until the desired formula or balance is reached. Just remember to keep in mind that selling investments can result in taxes unless they are held in a tax-free or advantaged account. Think 401k sponsored retirement plan or an IRA. So, just make sure the gains from sales outweigh the taxes or a profit can quickly become a loss or a break even.

The following list shows how many times during the past 30 years each type of investment has fared positively in terms of performance. It helps show why diversification among asset classes is important.

Asset class	Number of winning years, 1987-2016
Cash	3
Bonds	5

Everyman Investing

Stocks	10
Foreign stocks	12

Source: Thomson Reuters, 2017.

Simply stated a good portfolio (your collection of investments) allocation will balance your return with your risk. Risk, what is risk? I didn't sign up for that. Unfortunately, you did, as nothing in the stock market is risk-free. Not only can you fail to profit but you can also lose the money you initially invested if you make the wrong choices. But hey that is why we are only starting with $100 for this book. You will learn the best way to allocate your investments to make sure you are profiting year after year. In the following chapter, we explore basic strategies that fit most investors.

Proper Allocation

Basic Types of Allocations
<u>The Profit-Driven Portfolio</u>

This portfolio focuses on making money through alternative methods like dividends or distributions to stakeholders, in addition to capital gains from the stock price. These Blue-chip or more settled companies are usually not growth stocks, but I feel compelled to mention them as you may want to add some of them as your knowledge and investment skills grow. One bright side to value stocks it that you can continue to receive dividends from them in a downturn if the company's performance is stable. The income portfolio should generate positive cash flow, bottom line. This is real cash and profits in your pocket each year. Real Estate and Bonds are usually good options for this type of portfolio, in addition to companies that return a great majority of their profits back to shareholders instead of investing all of it in growing the business. They may invest some of it into the business, but the vast majority is written off by giving it to investors for tax benefits. In this way, they pass their income through to the shareholders and pay much fewer taxes. An example of this type of company is Real Estate Investment Trusts (REITs) which pool money to flip real estate, without one person taking all the risk. Most REITs are traded on major stock exchanges, but there are also public non-listed and private REITs. The two main types of REITs are equity REITs and mortgage REITs commonly known as mREITs, but there are four major types as shown below from Reit Invester.com

Equity REITs – a company that owns or operates income-producing real estate.

Mortgage REITs – mREITs provide financing for income-producing real estate by purchasing or originating mortgages and mortgage-backed securities and earning income from the interest on these investments.

Everyman Investing

Public Non-listed REITs – PNLRs are registered with the SEC but do not trade on any major stock exchanges.

Private REITs – Private REITs are offerings that are exempt from SEC registration and whose shares do not trade on national stock exchanges.

These stocks are very tied to the economic climate, even more than most stocks, but while the real estate market is hot or rising the profits from the resales are then given back to the investors as dividends. They can take a beating when the market falls, as real estate building and buying activity dries up. So, make sure you keep abreast of this as with any non-growth stock.

This Portfolio is a nice complement to most people's salary, wage, or retirement savings. Contrary to growth investors those in this type of portfolio should look out for stocks that may have fallen out of favor but still maintain a high rate of distributions to investors. These companies not only supplement income but also provide those capital gains, as no company pays dividends if its bottom line is not healthy. In addition to REITs, bonds, utilities, and other slow-growth industries are an ideal choice for this type of portfolio.

The Aggressive Portfolio

This portfolio is as close to Reno, Vegas, or Atlantic City as you can legally get. It presents more risk than any others we will discuss. Most experts say that a maximum of 10% of one's money be used to fund this type of portfolio. Aggressive stocks can be Initial Public Offerings (IPOs) of new companies, technology or health care businesses in the process of researching a breakthrough product, or a small energy company about to release its earnings report. Aggressive Portfolios and stocks, require the most work to be traded successfully, as you do not want to buy and hold but instead to use a day trading type of strategy.

An aggressive investment strategy is generally a strategy that is designed to maximize returns by taking a relatively higher degree of risk. Strategies for achieving higher returns typically emphasize growth over time as a primary investment goal, rather than steady income or safety of your principal. This strategy would, therefore, have an investment allocation with a substantial or majority percentage in stocks or real estate and little or no investments allocated to bonds or cash.

Aggressive investment strategies are generally more suitable for young adults with smaller portfolio sizes because they usually have a lengthy investment timeline that enables them to ride out short-term market changes. They are not deterred by sudden losses early on that may have less impact than changes near the end of the timeline. Most investment advisors do not consider this strategy right for anyone else unless such a strategy is applied to only a small portion of one's total savings. Regardless of the investor's age high tolerance to risk is a prerequisite for this type of strategy. These are the key concepts of an aggressive type allocation.

- Accepts more risk in pursuit of greater return.

- Achieves its goals through one or more of many strategies including asset selection and asset allocation.

Since the 2008 recession, data shows a preference away from aggressive strategies and active management and towards passive index investing. However, for those investing aggressively, their allocation would contain the following:

Portfolio One - 75% equities and real estate, 15% fixed income, and 10% commodities.

Portfolio Two - 85% equities and real estate and 15% commodities.

Aggressive investment strategies would also utilize a higher turnover strategy, seeking to concentrate on stocks that show high return in a short time period.

Generally, an aggressive strategy needs more constant management than a conservative long-term wait and hold strategy. It is likely to be much more volatile and could require a lot of adjustments, depending on market conditions. Also, more active rebalancing would also be required to bring portfolio allocations back to their target levels. The volatility of the assets could lead mixes to deviate significantly from their original weights.

The Mixed Portfolio

A mixed portfolio means venturing into other types of investments outside of stocks. Bonds, commodities, real estate, and even art. There is a lot of flexibility in this approach and a lot of people prefer it. Traditionally, this type of portfolio would contain growth and income stocks, government or corporate bonds, and REITs. A common strategy for a hybrid portfolio would include a mix of stocks and bonds in relatively fixed proportions. This type of approach offers diversification across multiple types of investments and is more suited for a conservative type of investor.

The best way to accomplish a mixed allocation would be to look at the timeline we have for when we might need the money we're investing. Any investors that might need their money within a year's time should simply invest in an interest-bearing cash account. Period. Taking a chance and investing your cash (when you need it so soon) in bonds or stocks is not advantageous as there is a huge chance that a percentage of your money could be lost before you need it. Keeping the principal safe and liquid is the smart thing to do for any money that might be needed quickly.

Money should be invested only if it's going toward long-term goals further than five years out, such as retirement. The best investment for long-term growth is stocks because, over long periods of time, they outperform nearly all other types of investments. This is even though they may lose value in a given year.

Many financial advisors adhere to the rule of subtracting your age from 110. The answer should be the percentage of your portfolio that's invested in stocks. As a person ages, their portfolio's mix of stocks and bonds will gradually move to a more conservative mix. Investors can always tweak the formula to their own tastes if they are willing to accept more risk. A more aggressive investor may up the number to 120, allowing a 50-year-old to invest 70% of their portfolio in stocks. Many investors and advisors believe that if they increase their portfolio's range of allocation and diversify its stock and other instruments, they decrease its risk. This is not necessarily true, especially for those who spend time studying individual investments. It can be safe to allocate your funds into a diverse range within the sale asset class. For example a mix of common and preferred stock or a range of different industries.

Now that you have an understanding of what a portfolio is and how to allocate it, let's take a look at the various strategies they most investors use.

Recession Proof Stocks

Yes, they exist and we are going to take a quick look at what makes a recession-proof stock and how to recognize them. First recession is defined as an extended period of time where the elements of economic growth are sub-par such as:

1. GDP (Gross Domestic Product)-In the 2006/8 recession the GDP defined as: private consumption + gross investment + government investment + government spending + (exports – imports), dipped with losses of 2.5% and finally started creeping up in 2009.

2. Unemployment Rate (number of unemployed persons / labor force)-The unemployment rate grew to 4.9% during the 2006 to 2008 recession and has steadily decreased to a low of 3.4% currently.

3. Job Creation (number of new job creation in comparison to the previous period)-In the 2006 to 2008 recession we lost almost 3 million jobs compared to the current rate of over 300k added per quarter.

4. Income Levels (rates of wages to inflation)-The rate of wages to inflation has remained at a steady 7.25 per hour for minimum wage in most states. The rate is low and is the subject of much debate.

5. Inflation Rate (value of the dollar to the cost of goods)- We have remained at the core rate of 1.9% for many

years with rates expected to climb to 2% in 2021 to 2022.

6. Strength of the Dollar (value of the dollar to other currencies)-The dollar has had a bit of roller coaster over the past 10 years, but still remains a powerful element in the world market.

With those ideas in mind, it is common sense that recession-proof stocks would be those that either assist "Main Street" with saving money or escaping the worry or stress that inevitably accompany a recession. Also, necessities like Food, Utilities, and basic transportation needs are pretty much recession proof. Here are the top recession-proof stocks that remained at least 2% (beating core inflation) growth during downturns:

- COSTCO (COST)-Current Stock Price-$243 per share, Lowest Price During Recession $189 per share

- Sam's Club and Walmart (WMT)-Current Stock Price-$102 per share, Lowest Price During Recession-$95 per share

- Walt Disney (DIS)-Current Stock Price-$133 per share, Lowest Price During Recession-$115 per share

- Netflix (NFLX)-Current Stock Price-$375 per share, Lowest Price During Recession-$325 per share

- Dollar General (DG)-Current Stock Price-$122 per share, Lowest Price During Recession-$115 per share

- Big Lots (BIG)-Current Stock Price-$37 per share, Lowest Price During Recession-$28 per share

- Spirit Airlines (SAVE)-Current Stock Price-$55 per share, Lowest Price During Recession-$50 per Share

- Molson Coors (TAP)-Current Stock Price-$60 per share, Lowest Price During Recession-$52 per share

- Constellation (marijuana) (STZ)-Current Stock Price-$205, Lowest Price During Recession (N/A)

- Canopy Growth (CGC)-Current Stock Price-$47 per share, Lowest Price During Recession (N/A)

- Cell Phone Carriers: T-Mobile (TMUS) Verizon (VZ) AT&T (T) Sprint (S) Current Stock Prices-73, 56, 31, & 5 per share, all of them held to at least 2% growth during 2006 to 2008

- Public Storage PSA S&P 500 lost 55% from 2007 - 2009; PSA shares lost 38%

- Brookfield Infrastructure Partners (BIP) S&P 500 lost 51% in 2008; BIP shares lost 43% (IPO'd in 2008)

Other stocks remained strong investments during the recession through the growth of their dividends:

- Duke Energy (DUK) S&P 500 lost 55% from 2007 - 2009; DUK shares lost 34%

  o Dividend Growth Streak: 11 years

- Digital Realty Trust (DLR) S&P 500 lost 55% from 2007 - 2009; DLR shares lost 27%

  o Dividend Growth Streak: 13 years

- WEC Energy Group (WEC) S&P 500 lost 55% from 2007 - 2009; WEC shares lost 18%

  o Dividend Growth Streak: 15 years

- Flowers Foods (FLO) S&P 500 lost 55% from 2007 - 2009; FLO shares lost 1%

  o Dividend Growth Streak: 16 years

- Magellan Midstream Partners (MMP) S&P 500 lost 55% from 2007 - 2009; MMP shares lost 30%

  o Dividend Growth Streak: 17 years

- Enterprise Products Partners (EPD) S&P 500 lost 55% from 2007 - 2009; EPD shares lost 37%

  o Dividend Growth Streak: 20 years

- Reality Income Corp (O) S&P 500 lost 55% from 2007 - 2009; O shares lost 43%

- o Dividend Growth Streak: 24 years

- Chevron (CVX) S&P 500 lost 55% from 2007 - 2009; CVX shares lost 34%

  - o Dividend Growth Streak: 32 years

- Exxon Mobil Corporation (XOM) S&P 500 lost 55% from 2007 - 2009; XOM shares lost 28%

  - o Dividend Growth Streak: 35 years

- Consolidated Edison (ED) S&P 500 lost 55% from 2007 - 2009; ED shares lost 26%

  - o Dividend Growth Streak: 44 years

- Pepsico (PEP) S&P 500 lost 55% from 2007 - 2009; PEP shares lost 35%

  - o Dividend Growth Streak: 45 years

- Kimberly-Clark (KMB) S&P 500 lost 55% from 2007 - 2009; KMB shares lost 34%

  - o Dividend Growth Streak: 45 years

- Leggett & Platt (LEG) S&P 500 lost 55% from 2007 - 2009; LEG shares lost 44%

  - o Dividend Growth Streak: 46 years

- Altria (MO) S&P 500 lost 55% from 2007 - 2009; MO

shares lost 20%

- Dividend Growth Streak: 49 years

- Coca-Cola (KO) S&P 500 lost 55% from 2007 - 2009; KO shares lost 31%

    - Dividend Growth Streak: 55 years

- Johnson & Johnson (JNJ) S&P 500 lost 55% from 2007 - 2009; JNJ shares lost 27%

    - Dividend Growth Streak: 56 years

- Procter & Gamble (PG) S&P 500 lost 55% from 2007 - 2009; PG shares lost 36%

    - Dividend Growth Streak: 61 years

Do you see the pattern of necessity and escape in these stocks? Keep that in mind during the next downturn with the noted characteristics of these types of stocks:

1. *The company provides critical repair/maintenance/essentials-*Consumers cut out optional services first and identify things they can do themselves instead of hiring them out. Think about household repairs, landscaping, or house cleaning.

2. *The company serves an elite or protected client-*These are both the very rich who will continue their luxuries and those somewhat protected from the recession.

Think food delivery to grocers, supplies to utility plants, and medical and pharmaceutical suppliers.

3. *The company provides products or services that are the rule of law-*They provide their services or products to people or business that run under a government mandate. Think police, fire, EMS and those that supply them, and the military.

4. *The Company provides escape or needed stress relief-*This seems trivial, but alcohol, marijuana, and home-based entertainment companies usually remain stable during times of recession. See the above list of recession-proof stocks for examples.

5. *The company provides discounted essentials or is built on bargains-*Think stores and businesses that are known for providing cheap or heavily discounted products. The list of stocks above represents discount retailers and travel providers.

Source: Investopedia

The Basic Investment Strategies

1. Value Investing

   This is the investment strategy we looked at in chapter two which is based on finding stocks that are underpriced or undervalued. The amount of chart reading and research this takes is staggering and the returns can be very slow. This a buy and hold that requires a long-term investor who is content with holding onto a stock for years to get a payoff.

2. Income or Profit Investing

    This strategy involves going heavy into Profit Stocks/Portfolios that involve companies that pay distributions and capital gains on resale price. They can provide a reliable income stream with minimal risk and because they are a long term hold and should comprise at least a small portion of every investment strategy.

3. Growth Investing

    This investment strategy focuses on capital appreciation by looking for companies that exhibit signs of above-average growth, even if the share price appears expensive in terms of metrics. This strategy is somewhat riskier and involves investing in smaller companies that have a large potential for growth in growth sectors.

4. Small Cap/Micro Cap Investing

    This is for those looking to take on a little more risk in their portfolio. As the name gives away, a small-cap investor focuses on purchasing stocks from small companies who are relatively unknown and thus less expensive. Often referred to as "Penny Stocks", they are companies with very cheap prices that the investor feels are poised to grow exponentially. Bigger companies can have inflated prices since everyone's paying attention to them, while small-cap stocks tend to have fewer people that even know about them. Less risky investors stay away from them due to the risk and most group investors (mutual funds) have restrictions when it comes to investing in them. They are more volatile and therefore difficult to trade.

Whatever you decide, just remember that your goal is a balanced approach with an initial emphasis on Growth Stocks and Investing until you learn the ropes. Then you can enter into more difficult strategies. A balanced investment strategy aims to be more middle of the road and tends to meet the needs of most investors. Its goal is to balance your risk with return and seeks to create a portfolio you are comfortable with.

For example, ask yourself the following when choosing a strategy:

1. Are you wanting to preserve your capital/initial investment?

2. Do you want aggressive or fast returns?

3. Do you want steady income?

4. How long are you willing to let the money remain invested?

Even a balanced investment strategy can be rather aggressive in nature for some and is more suitable for those investors with at least five years to wait for returns. It is very appropriate for a younger investor, who has many more years to work and retirement is a distant goal. If you have a much shorter time frame in mind or a different type of goal that will occur in less than five years, a big purchase (home or vehicle) for instance, you may want to concentrate on a more conservative strategy and focus on the preservation of capital.

Preservation of capital focuses on maintaining current capital levels and preventing/limiting loss. This strategy works mainly with short term and secure investments like government bonds or Certificate of Deposits. A capital preservation strategy will work for older investors or those needing their money for a life event in less than five years. It is for those looking to maximize their current financial assets and to avoid taking significant risks with their chunk of money.

If you are young or have 10 plus years or more to play with a chunk of money you may want to consider an aggressive strategy that maximizes growth, while not concentrating too much on risk. These type of strategy would focus on a portfolio that centers on small-cap stocks, corporate bonds, junk bonds (below investment grade), FOREX (world currencies), real estate, and cryptocurrency. In general, a capital growth portfolio will contain majority stocks and bonds with a smaller amount in currency/real estate and the final bit in cash or even precious metals. Growth-oriented strategies seek high returns by definition, the mixture still protects the investor somewhat from losses on a larger scale while not concentrating too much on a small daily loss.

Why Growth Stocks to Start?

Well from the research we have done it is clear that as a new investor you want to cut your teeth on the simplest type of investment which, for someone with more than 5 years to play with, is Growth Investing. It requires the least amount of research and can yield the greatest returns over time. In fact, a simple Google Search can tell you what companies fall into this category. Simply Google:

1. Growth Industries

2. Best Stocks in the Industry

3. That company's income statements

Remember a growth stock is a share in a company that has shown faster or greater than average growth and has the potential to continue growing faster than the overall economy. The one drawback of these stocks is that because

69

such stocks generally increase in price quicker and in a higher percentage than other stocks, they cost an average of 25% more per share than a value stock. The rapid growth is usually based on the company's current earnings and projected growth over the next 5 to 10 years. In the long run, the price you would pay for the stock is usually justified, but they also tend to be considered a riskier investment.

If a company shows stability or growth over the past 5 years, it is definitely a growth stock, but to make things easier I have compiled a detailed list of the top 100 growth stocks and how they stand at the time of publication in the next section of the book. Read on for the in-depth information.

Chapter Four Growth Stocks Part 1

Baidu (NASDAQ: BIDU)

Price at time of writing: $165.72 USD

Often dubbed the "Google of China", the Chinese search engine and online advertising leader suffered a 32% dip in 2018, but now looks like the share price has finally reached the bottom.

Chinese ad spending increased 25% year on year, and Baidu still controls roughly 70% of the online advertising space. This isn't showing any signs of slowing down either. In addition to this, the company is investing heavily in Internet of Things (IoT) technology and cloud computing, two more growth markets.

Financials are solid and third quarter sales increased by 27% on a year-on-year period.

Baidu's hidden gem is its strong relationship with the Chinese government. This is vital for any China-based stock as centralization still heavily dominates the business scene.

The big risk here is that Google makes a play to re-enter the Chinese market, which could signal the end of Baidu as the consensus number one. However, Google has tried and failed before to dominate the world's largest country.

This stock isn't for everyone, with any Chinese based stock, you must be willing to bear more volatility, but if there's a space in your portfolio for a potentially explosive growth play, Baidu is a great option.

Horizon Pharma (NASDAQ: HZNP)

Price at time of writing: $24.88 USD

Founded in 2005, this Irish Based Pharma Company in Dublin, Ireland was relocated to Chicago, IL USA. Its specialization was and remains pain and anti-inflammatory remedies.

97% of the company's sales are to US medical companies and doctors, hence the move to the states to save on shipping costs.

Current sales stand at $1.056 billion per year with the vast majority coming from outside Ireland and the European Area.

Horizon's strengths are in its strong relationship with the USA and North American Market and its recent acquisitions of smaller Pharma companies (Raptor & Hyperion) with their patented Arthritis drugs, Procysbi and Quinsar. This gives them a substantial share in the pain management sector.

The main risks are the large amount of publicity related to the opioid crisis and the loss of patents, but as it stands it is poised for growth in the next 5 to 10 years.

This stock will remain fairly stable even in a downturn so it is appropriate for all investors.

Okta (NASDAQ: OKTA)

Price at time of writing: $99.73 USD

Founded in 1978 in the Balkan Country of Macedonia. Okta is part of the Hellenic Petroleum Group and is one of the biggest providers of fossil-based fuels and cloud software which helps companies manage and secure user authentication into modern applications in the world.

Current sales stand at $7.80 billion per year with product distribution all over the world, especially in Europe.

OTKA's strength is in its strong relationship with the Greek Government. Indeed, this company was owned by the government up until recently when they began transitioning to a private firm.

The main risk is the large amount of attention given to switching away from fossil fuel dependency and onto renewable sources of fuel. However, its other emphasis on cloud technologies will keep it solid.

This stock will remain fairly stable even in a downturn as it provides essential services and is beginning to look at green fuels production.

Everyman Investing

The fact it is linked to volatile Balkan areas may yield dips and rises more than the average investor would like, but overall it is appropriate for the long hold investor.

W.W. Grainger (NASDAQ: GWW)

Price at time of writing: $292.74 USD

Founded in 1927 in Chicago, IL this company is one of the largest suppliers of industrial supplies to factories, retailers, and construction sites. They currently have over 900 US locations and almost 100 Canadian.

Current sales stand at $10.4 billion with distribution all over the world, the majority of which remains within North America.

Its strengths are in its great reputation and history of stellar service, as well as relationships with the majority of retailers and big construction companies.

The main risks are the large stakes it has in commercial construction which slow during a downturn, but it has a healthy enough maker share with governments and retail that it has remained strong during both a depression and recession.

This stock will remain fairly stable even in a downturn as it provides essential services/products.

The fact it is linked to essential service and has a longstanding history makes it an appropriate stock for most growth investors.

West Pharmaceutical Services (NASDAQ: WST)

Price at time of writing: $115.55 USD

Founded in 1923 in Exton, PA, West Pharmaceutical Services is a designer and manufacturer of pharmaceutical packaging and delivery systems. It is one of the USA's largest producers and designers of prescription/OTC medicines and medical devices, as well as medicinal distribution and delivery of drugs.

Current sales stand at $1.7 billion per year with distribution all over the world.

Its strengths are in its strong ties to American medical companies and providers and the fact that its products are some of the most essential services. An additional strength is its great distribution chain serving Europe and the Far East, as well as North America.

It maintains average risk with the expiration of patents, but West remains a strong company for the future.

This stock will remain fairly stable even in a downturn as it provides essential services.

The fact it is linked to very stable areas will make it a good investment for most investors.

Everyman Investing

Alibaba (NASDAQ: BABA)

Price at time of writing: $187.37 USD

Founded in 1919 in the Alibaba Group at Xixi in Hangzhou, China, Alibaba is a Chinese multinational conglomerate specializing in e-commerce, retail, internet, and technology. It is one of China's largest consumer, electronics, retail, and payment providers. Think of it as the Amazon/PayPal of China.

Current sales stand at $250 Billion per year with distribution all over the world.

Its strengths are in its strong ties the Chinese Government and the fact its products make up the majority of Far East consumer products and electronic payments. Another significant strength is its great distribution chain serving the Far East

It maintains average risk despite the emerging competition in the space due to its strong sales topping Walmart, eBay, and Amazon Combined in 2015. This stock will remain fairly stable even in a downturn. Also, complaints from Western companies about substandard products will limit exposure in the West.

The fact it is linked to high sales and has a sort of monopoly in this location makes it a good fit for most investors that do not mind the volatility of the Far East.

PayPal (NASDAQ: PYPL)

Price at time of writing: $106.93 USD

Founded in 1998 in Silicon Valley, CA. It started as a subsidiary of eBay to process its payments. It became a universal payment process as an independent company in 2014.

Current sales stand at $13.9 Billion per year with users all over the world.

Its strengths are in its strong ties to the major online retailers with which it works. With online transactions making up over 70% of all transactions. In addition to online dominance, PayPal has negotiated contracts with traditional retailers and individuals for payment for service. It is a top five method of payment all over the world.

It maintains average risk with the emerging competition with retailers and individuals. PayPal continues to expand where it is taken by purchasing European payment processors like IZettle. This stock will remain fairly stable even in a downturn as money transfer is essential.

The fact it is linked to high sales and has a sort of monopoly on payment options allows it to remain strong and ideal for all investors.

Everyman Investing

Amazon (NASDAQ: AMZN)

Price at time of writing: $1927.39 USD

Founded in 1994 in Seattle, WA Amazon is a technology company that focuses on e-commerce, payment processing, cloud computing, and artificial intelligence. Amazon is the largest e-commerce marketplace and cloud computing platform in the world as measured by revenue and market capitalization. They started as a small online bookseller, but eventually expanded to become the go-to online retailer selling most consumer products and electronics. In the later 2000's it expanded into Fresh Grocery delivery by acquiring Whole Foods, AI with Alexia, and credit by partnering with several banks for credit cards, as well as expanding into Video Streaming/Production and on-demand delivery with Prime and Prime Now.

Current sales stand at $233 billion per year and climbing with users all over the world. It is by far the world's biggest retailer and shows no signs of slowing down. The main drawback is the recent allegations about employee abuse and employment violations. This seems to have been lingering for a number of years, but has died down a bit and has not caused any dip in business.

Its strengths are in its strong ties to multiple industries and its reputation as a bargain place to shop with free delivery.

It maintains average risk with the emerging competition with other retailers and tech companies. This stock will remain fairly stable even in a downturn as it sells many essentials and will be on the front lines of Finance, AI, and Cloud Computing.

The fact that it is linked to high sales and has a partial monopoly on sales allows it to remain strong and ideal for all investors.

Carvana (NASDAQ: CVNA)

Price at time of writing: $67.05 USD

Founded in 2013 in Tempe, AZ as a subsidiary of DriveTime, Carvana became independent in 2014. It started as an online car and parts retailer, but eventually expanded to become a one-stop shop for used vehicles. It is a unique experience that allows shoppers to order, customize, and finance a car for delivery or purchase from their vehicle vending machines at their physical locations.

Current sales stand at $20 million per year and climbing with online and store sales.

Its strengths are in its unique experience as an online car superstore and its vending machine option is a huge attraction if only for the novelty.

It maintains average risk with the emerging competition with other retailers and tech companies. However, this stock will remain fairly stable even in a downturn as it sells cars for rock bottom prices.

The fact that it is a low price leader will keep this a stable stock for most investors.

TriNet Group (NASDAQ: TNET)

Price at time of writing: $62.37 USD

Founded in 1988 in San Leandro, CA as a payroll provider but later expanded to become a one-stop shop for all things payroll and HR, TriNet provides important tasks for small to medium-sized companies that would normally be handled by an in-house employee for a lot less money.

Current sales stand at $3.5 billion per year and climbing as more companies outsource this type of work.

Its strengths are in its reputation and the statistics that say over 75% of companies outsource HR and payroll.

It maintains average risk with the emerging competition with other companies, but the fact it has a longstanding reputation with many established companies are in its favor.

The fact that it is an industry leader will keep this a stable stock for most investors.

Canopy Growth Corp (NASDAQ: CGC)

Price at time of writing: $47.73 USD

Canopy Growth Corp was formerly Tweed Marijuana Inc. and is a cannabis company based in Smiths Falls, Ontario. Tweed was founded by Bruce Linton and Chuck Rifici in 2013 and renamed Canopy Growth Corporation in 2015. Since its inception in 2013, the company has remained in Ontario, Canada as one of a handful of Cannabis Companies present at the time. Canopy Growth Corp still owns over 30% of the market share.

Current sales stand at $40 million per year and climbing as the Cannabis industry expands at a rapid rate.

Its strengths are in its reputation and the fact that it was one for the first legalized producers.

It maintains average risk despite the emerging competition with other companies, especially since many countries and states still have not legalized cannabis yet. CGC remains poised as a leader as any competition will take many years to get established.

The fact it is an industry leader will keep this a stable stock for most that have no moral conflicts with investing in marijuana.

Square (NASDAQ: SQ)

Price at time of writing: $72.46 USD

Everyman Investing

Founded in 2009 in San Francisco, CA as one of less than 5 point of sale services for individuals and small businesses. Its square reader accepts credit card payments by connecting to a mobile device's audio jack. The original version consisted of a simple read head directly wired to a 3.5 mm audio jack but has expanded into having its own range of full Point of Sale units for businesses.

Current sales stand at $4.5 billion per year and climbing as the premier payment processor of small business and individual proprietors. Its strengths are in its reputation and the fact that it has become synonymous with taking payments- "we've got a square".

It maintains average risk with the emerging competition with other companies, and the fact remains that it is poised as a leader and any others have to play catch up at this point.

The fact it is an industry leader will keep this a stable stock for most investors and it has the potential to go as high as the tech sector.

Control4 (NASDAQ: CTRL)

Price at time of writing: $17.45 USD

Founded in 2003 in Draper, UT, Control4 is a leading global provider of automation, AI, surveillance, and networking for homes and businesses. It offers personalized control of lighting, music, video, comfort, security, and communications integrated into a unified smart home system that enhances the daily lives of its consumers by allowing them to control all aspects of their home from their table, computer, or smartphone. Its main product functions as a creator and designer of automation and networking systems for homes and businesses. It literally joins the multiple networks of single buildings together to allow its residents to do everything seamlessly and without extra effort or the click of a button remotely.

Current sales stand at $15.5 billion per year and climbing as the premier provider of "smart building technology". Its focus is on both on its products and infrastructure.

It maintains average risk with the emerging competition with other companies, but the fact remains that it is poised as a leader and any others have to play catch up at this point.

The fact it is an industry leader will keep this a stable stock for most investors and it has the potential to go as high as the AI sector.

Voyager Therapeutics (NASDAQ: VYGR)

Price at time of writing: $20.75 USD

Everyman Investing

Voyager Therapeutics is developing life-changing gene therapies focused on severe neurological diseases. Diseases like Parkinson's disease, Huntington's disease, Alzheimer's disease, and other neurodegenerative diseases. They were founded in 2000 by a group of neuroscientists and researchers.

Current sales stand at $12 billion per year and climbing one of the leaders in the biotech field.

Its strengths are in relationships with some of the foremost research facilities in the world.

It maintains low to average risk with the emerging competition with other companies, but the fact remains that it is still the definitive leader in the neurological area and any others have lots of research to do to catch up.

The fact it is an industry leader will keep this a stable stock for most investors and it has the potential to go as high as the tech sector.

Kinross Gold (NASDAQ: KGC)

Price at time of writing: $3.15 USD

Founded in 1993 in Toronto Ontario, Canada as one the best miners of gold and silver in North America. It currently operates eight active gold mines and was ranked fourth of the

"10 Top Gold-mining Companies" of 2017 by several business publications.

Current sales stand at $3.3 million per year and climbing as one of the last full-scale extractors of precious metals. The gold and silver industries have remained stable and Kinross will continue to be one of the only players in town to do the job.

It maintains above average risk with the shrinkage of the mining industry in general, but as one of less than a handful of players, it will keep its market share. The very cheap price is one that should be bought in bulk while the price is low.

The fact it is an industry leader will keep this a stable stock for most investors and it has the potential.

Mitsubishi (NASDAQ: MSBHY)

Price at time of writing: $54.57 USD

Founded in 1871 as a manufacturer of Japanese Steamboats, no company on this list is older than Mitsubishi, it has been through several alterations and evolutions during its long history. From steamboats to insurance and then to weapons for the Japanese War effort, before it was finally revamped as a car manufacturer in the 1950s. It still remains very diverse today and is on the cutting edge of all its industries. It is the sixth-largest Japanese automaker and the nineteenth-largest worldwide by production standards. Since 2016, Mitsubishi has been almost one-third (34%) owned by Nissan and is now a part of the Renault–Nissan–Mitsubishi Alliance.

Current sales stand at $552 billion per year and climbing as its flexes it muscles across all of the following by focusing on various sectors within its industry. Some of its work includes computer/processing technology, transportation, water, electricity and industrial projects; asset management, asset financing, real estate and logistics; investment in all forms of energy including fossil fuels and renewable energy; precious metals and industrial raw ingredients; manufacturing of many types of vehicles including cars and military; and consumer products.

Its strengths are in its diversification and solid reputation across all its sectors.

It maintains low risk with the emerging competition with other companies, and the fact remains that it is hard to compete with based on size alone.

The fact it is an industry leader will keep this a stable stock for most investors and it has the potential to go as high as any of its sectors.

Vanda Pharmaceuticals (NASDAQ: VNDA)

Price at time of writing: $17.31 USD

Founded in 1999 in Germany as one of the few leaders in what are considered unmet medical needs in the areas of sleep deprivation and schizophrenia. Its drugs for these ailments are its premier products.

Current sales stand at $225 million per year and climbing as much as 17% year by year as the number one producer of mental health medicines related to mood and sleep.

It maintains low risk with the emerging competition with other companies, as few show any interest competing for its niche market share.

The fact it is an industry leader will keep this a stable stock for most investors and it has the potential to go as high as the biotech sector.

XPO Logistics (NASDAQ: XPO)

Price at time of writing: $67.05 USD

Founded in 1989 in Greenwich CE as a simple trucking company. Today XPO logistics operates in 32 countries and is the preferred logistics company for 67 of the Forbes Fortune 100 companies. It is one of the world's 10 largest providers of transportation and logistics services. XPO operates as a third-party provider in over 25 countries and has over 35,000 customers, including 70 of the Fortune 100.

Everyman Investing

Current sales stand at $17 billion per year and climbing as the premier delivery and freight company of the elites of business. It is also heavily investing in the future by working with Tesla to test the autonomous trucks and with other AI companies for Smart Distribution Centers, so it is poised for the future.

It maintains average risk with the emerging competition with other companies, but the fact remains that it is poised as a leader with deep connections to those that need their services.

The fact it is an industry leader will keep this a stable stock for most investors and it has the potential to go as high as the logistics sector.

HubSpot (NASDAQ: HUBS)

Price at time of writing: $166.23 USD

Founded in 2005 at MIT in Boston, HubSpot remains a leader in software and cloud computing solutions for social media and online advertising in general.

Current sales stand at $553 million per year and climbing as the supplier of advertising products on Facebook, Instagram, and Twitter. This is in addition to the software it provided for SEO optimization and Adwords Searches.

It maintains average risk with the emerging competition with other companies, there are very few that can turn out the number of quality products and establish the partnership with Google and Facebook that HubSpot already has.

The fact it is an industry leader will keep this a stable stock for most investors and it has the potential to go as high as the tech sector.

Veeva Systems (NASDAQ: VEEV)

Price at time of writing: $136.57 USD

Founded in 2007 in Pleasanton, CA. It is one of the few in the burgeoning industry crossover of biotech and cloud computing. It develops and services software that aids in cutting edge life science research across the globe.

Current sales stand at $100 billion per year and climbing as the premier supplier and creator of software that organizes and services the top researchers in the life, environmental, and medical fields.

It maintains low risk as emerging competition is low in the niche, and the fact remains that it is poised as a leader and any others have to play catch up at this point.

The fact it is an industry leader will keep this a stable stock for most investors and it has the potential to go as high as the tech sector.

Adobe (NASDAQ: ADBE)

Price at time of writing: $278.49 USD

Founded in 1982 in San Jose, CA as a creative software company. Adobe primarily focuses on the creation of multimedia and creativity software products, with a more recent foray towards digital marketing software.

Current sales stand at $9.3 billion per year and climbing as the premier creator and marketer of creative and not marketing software.

It maintains low risk despite the emerging competition with other companies due to the solid grip it has on the industry.

The fact it is an industry leader will keep this a stable stock for most investors and it has the potential to go as high as the tech sector.

Cerner Corp. (NASDAQ: CERN)

Price at time of writing: $63.83 USD

Founded in 1979 in Kansas City, MO as a provider of healthcare IT (HIT) software, hardware, and medical devices. Cerner Corporation is a supplier of health information technology solutions, services, devices, and hardware. Its products are in use at more than 25,000 facilities around the world. The company has more than 30,000 employees globally, with over 12,000 in its HQ in Kansas City, Missouri.

Current sales stand at $5.3 billion per year and climbing as the premier provider of HIT-related gadgets and tools to the vast majority of US and European Medical Companies.

It maintains low risk despite the emerging competition as it is generally well connected with the decision makers in the medical industry and provides stellar service and quality.

The fact it is an industry leader will keep this a stable stock for most investors and it has the potential to go as high as the bio sector.

Salesforce (NASDAQ: CRM)

Price at time of writing: $161.23 USD

Founded in 1999 in San Francisco, CA as a provider of client management and scheduling software. It has expanded to a 95% cloud-based system that primarily works with sales and service companies in the realm of client management and sales tracking. Its main product is a cloud computing service as a software (SaaS) company that specializes in customer relationship management (CRM). The software is number one for customer success and helps businesses track customer activity, sales, revenues, market to customers, and many more elements involved in customer management.

Current sales stand at $10.48 billion per year and climbing as the premier provider of sales and client tracking software and cloud-based systems. It also provides analytics, customer service, and data tracking software.

It maintains low risk despite the emerging competition in this sector as many are trying to break in this wide open niche. However, the fact remains that it is poised as a leader and any others have to play catch up at this point.

The fact it is an industry leader will keep this a stable stock for most investors and it has the potential to go as high as the tech sector.

CSX Corp. (NASDAQ: CSX)

Price at time of writing: $79.02 USD

Founded in 1980 in Jacksonville FL as a provider of rail and railroad equipment for the vast train logistics chains across the USA. Presently it has expanded into heavy equipment for industrial use and real estate holdings.

Current sales stand at $5.4 billion per year and climbing as the provider for the railroad industry and industrial real estate.

It maintains low risk with very little competition in its areas of interest and is poised for a bright future in the industry. It has invested in smart warehouse and smart car technologies that will make it the forerunner for the future of the mass transit sector.

The fact it is an industry leader will keep this a stable stock for most investors and it has the potential to go as high as the logistics sector.

Activision Blizzard (NASDAQ: ATVI)

Price at time of writing: $46.51 USD

Activision was founded in 2008 in Santa Monica, CA as a producer of film, video, and video games. Among its most popular titles are Treyarch, Infinity Ward, High Moon Studios and Toys for Bob, Call of Duty, Guitar Hero, Tony Hawk's, and Spyro/Skylanders through Activision's studios, as well as World of Warcraft, StarCraft, Diablo, Candy Crush Saga, Hearthstone, and Overwatch.

Current sales stand at $7.5 billion per year and climbing as Activision continues to release new games and update the most popular ones with new releases. In 2018, its release of Call of Duty: Black Ops 4 and its re-release of the popular game is Candy Crush Saga are just a few examples of successful new games.

Everyman Investing

It maintains average risk with the emerging competition with other companies, but the fact remains that it is the creator of some of the most popular titles in the history of gaming and it will remain a leader in the industry. The only wild card is the recently proposed regulations on the practice of microtransactions both in free games and purchased games. Within the realm of free games (like Activision's Candy Crush or Hearthstone) players are charged a few cents for advanced tactics, weapons, or tools. It is generally the only way these games make money, but the problem is that the practice has extended to paid games. This happens when you are charged money in game for more weapons/updates/designs. This resulted in many complaints and bills are being proposed to limit this. We predict no big issues, but it is something to watch.

The fact it is an industry leader will keep this a stable stock for most investors and it has the potential to go as high as the tech sector.

Expedia Group (NASDAQ: EXPE)

Price at time of writing: $125.88 USD

Founded in 1996 in Bellevue, WA as a part of Microsoft, Expedia is currently one of the largest providers of travel software and booking platforms in the world. It owns the well-known names of Hotels.com, Expedia, Travelocity, CarRentals.com, CheapTickets, HomeAway, Hotwire.com, Orbitz, Travelocity, Trivago, and Venere.com.

Current sales stand at $10.5 billion per year and climbing as the provider of the most travel booking services in the world. It has partnerships with many airlines, hotels, car rentals companies, and other leisure providers. It has the strength of exclusive cheap pricing and an excellent reputation for service.

It maintains a very low risk with the emerging competition as there is very little of it, as Expedia has the partnerships to remain the industry leader. In short, Expedia competes only with itself in this industry.

The fact it is an industry leader will keep this a stable stock for most investors and it has the potential to go as high as the tech and travel sector.

Everyman Investing

Chapter Five Growth Stocks Part 2

Emerson Electric (NASDAQ: EMR)

Price at time of writing: $73.16 USD

Founded in 1890 and currently residing in Ferguson, MO (outside St. Louis), Emerson Electric is a provider of engineering services to major manufacturers and utilities across the USA.

Current sales stand at $15.6 billion per year and climbing as the premier provider of engineering, maintenance, and support services to public utilities and manufacturers.

It maintains low risk with very little competition in the area and is poised for a bright future in the industry. Its strong relationships with many essential service providers make it strong even in a downturn.

The fact that it is an industry leader will keep this a stable stock for most investors and it has the potential to go as high as the logistics/engineering sector.

Wynn Resorts (NASDAQ: WYNN)

Price at time of writing: $143.44 USD

Founded in 2002 and currently residing in Los Vegas, NV, Wynn Resorts is a provider of gambling, entertainment, and leisure across many properties in the Western and Eastern portions of the USA. One of its major properties opened during the 2006 recession and maintained decent profits, so they are in it for the long haul.

Current sales stand at $4.4 billion per year and climbing as the premier provider of leisure services.

It maintains low risk due to the strong ties to state gaming commissions and Native American Tribes that manage many of its properties. Its strong relationship with the aforementioned entities allows it to remain strong even in a downturn.

The fact it is an industry leader will keep this a stable stock for most investors and it has the potential to go as high as the gaming sector.

Crocs (NASDAQ: CROX)

Price at time of writing: $26.85 USD

Founded in 2002 and currently residing in Boulder, CO, Crocs is a provider of footwear and apparel for men, women, and children. Originally founded to make light foam shoes for boaters and fishermen.

Current sales stand at $1 billion per year and climbing as the brand has caught on with the general public and has found their way into the pop culture.

It maintains low risk with very little competition within its niche and is poised for a bright future in the industry. Its strong relationships with many huge retailers and brand loyalty from its wearers confer strength to its position in the market.

The fact it is an industry leader will keep this a stable stock for most investors and it has the potential to go as high as the clothing sector.

Twilio (NASDAQ: TWLO)

Price at time of writing: $130.23 USD

Founded in 2008 and currently residing in San Francisco, CA, Twilio is a provider of web-based communication to businesses and allows the use of its APIs to complete a variety of communications like texts/calls via their databases. It is very comparable to Slack and Skype and has excelled in partnering with other top companies such as LuLulemon. Twilio supports the development of open-source software and regularly makes contributions to the open-source community. They recently launched OpenVBX, an open-source product that lets business users configure phone numbers to receive and route phone calls. It also sponsors Localtunnel which enables software developers to expose their local development environment to the public internet. The fact that it supports open source makes it a darling of the tech world.

Current sales stand at $650 million per year and climbing as the premier provider of these services to major companies and government entities.

It maintains low risk with very little competition in the area and is poised for a bright future in the industry. Its strong relationships with many large companies and its cutting edge research to improve its communication system are key to keeping it strong.

The fact it is an industry leader will keep this a stable stock for most investors and it has the potential to go as high as the tech sector.

LuLulemon (NASDAQ: LULU)

Price at time of writing: $176.17 USD

Founded in 1998 and currently residing in Vancouver BC, Canada, Lululemon is a provider of athletic apparel for women and men. It has evolved from an athletic brand into a designer brand known for comfort, style, and quality.

Current sales stand at $2.6 billion per year and climbing as it has become a high fashion brand with a thriving resale market online.

Everyman Investing

It maintains low risk with very little competition as its resellers and those that wear it are fiercely loyal. In addition, the fact that a garment can last years, even under high use makes it a good fit for those looking to get the most for their money.

The fact it is an industry leader will keep this a stable stock for most investors and it has the potential to go as high as the designer/athletic clothing sectors.

MongoDB (NASDAQ: MDB)

Price at time of writing: $136.97 USD

Founded in 2007 and currently residing in NY, NY, MongoDB is a provider of database management services in a cloud environment to millions of users. It allows businesses to manage their own database of information, without having to maintain servers and other bulky items.

Current sales stand at $25 billion per year and climbing as the premier provider of data management for a host of retailers, companies, and small businesses.

It maintains low risk with very little competition in the area and is poised for a bright future in the industry. Its strong relationships with many businesses and stellar track record for service and research will keep it strong.

The fact it is an industry leader will keep this a stable stock for most investors and it has the potential to go as high as the logistics/engineering sector.

Sarepta Therapeutics (NASDAQ: SRPT)

Price at time of writing: $116.86 USD

Founded in 1980 in Cambridge, MA, Sarepta Therapeutics is a provider of research and pharmaceuticals geared toward anti-viral treatments and respiratory ailments. Some of its major products are known for treating West Nile Virus, Hepatitis, and Pneumonia.

Current sales stand at $5.5 billion per year and climbing as the premier provider of these drugs to hospitals, clinics, and medical professionals.

It maintains low risk with he very little competition in the area and is poised for a bright future in the industry. Its strong reputation with respiratory and viral research will make it a leader for many years.

The fact it is an industry leader will keep this a stable stock for most investors and it has the potential to go as high as the biotech sector.

Everyman Investing

Netflix (NASDAQ: NFLX)

Price at time of writing: $377.23 USD

Founded in 1997 in Los Gatos, CA, Netflix began with mail-order DVD rentals and has since morphed into the leader in digital streaming and a provider of original movies and programming.

Current sales stand at $15.7 billion per year and climbing as the premier provider of these services worldwide. Recently released financial statements show consistent growth from month to month, indicating that its business model is effective.

It maintains low risk with very little competition in the niche of the one-stop streaming shop and an independent studio. The only other platforms close are HULU and AMAZON, but the former's ties to cable TV and the latter's emphasis on retail rather than streaming makes Netflix the clear winner. Netflix is poised for a bright future in the industry. Its strong relationship with many large companies and its cutting edge research to improve its communication system are key to keeping it strong.

The fact it is an industry leader will keep this a stable stock for most investors and it has the potential to go as high as the tech sector.

Qualcomm (NASDAQ: QCOM)

Price at time of writing: $88.10 USD

Founded in 1985 in San Diego, CA, Qualcomm is a provider of semiconductor and wireless communications equipment worldwide. They provide the guts that make the wireless data market work such as towers, antennas, and fiber optics.

Current sales stand at $22.7 billion per year and climbing as the premier provider of these services to major companies and government entities.

It maintains low risk with very little competition in the area and is poised for a bright future in the industry. Its strong relationship with many large companies and its cutting edge research to improve its systems and keep up with every generation of wireless data are fundamental to its strong position in the industry.

The fact it is an industry leader will keep this a stable stock for most investors and it has the potential to go as high as the tech sector.

Alphabet Inc. (NASDAQ: GOOGLE)

Price at time of writing: $12733.88 USD

Founded in 2015 and currently residing in Mountain View,

CA, Alphabet Inc. is the parent company of Google which is the number one search engine in the world. In addition, they own YouTube the 2nd largest search engine, as well as being the go-to company for advertising, research, and AI.

Current sales stand at $136 billion per year and climbing as the premier provider of these services to major companies, individuals, and government entities.

It maintains low risk with very little competition in the area and is poised for a bright future in the industry. Its strong relationship with many large companies and its cutting edge research to improve its market reach is key to keeping it strong.

The fact it is an industry leader will keep this a stable stock for most investors and it has the potential to go as high as the tech sector.

iRobot (NASDAQ: IRBT)

Price at time of writing: $103.36 USD

Founded in 1990 by 3 MIT students in Cambridge, MA and currently residing in Bedford, MA, iRobot is a provider of AI-based home products like the Roomba. It is also developing a line of police, fire protection, and military robots. It has an exclusive agreement with the military for battle robots and is the largest provider of personal robots in the world, the most commonly known of which is the Roomba.

Current sales stand at $1.79 billion per year and climbing as the premier provider of these products to the military and individuals.

It maintains low risk with very little competition in the area of homes based AI gadgets and is poised for a bright future in the industry. Its strong relationship with many large retailers and its cutting edge research to improve its products and expand its offerings into the new sector of smart homes will keep iRobot a strong player in the industry.

The fact it is an industry leader will keep this a stable stock for most investors and it has the potential to go as high as the tech and AI sector.

Facebook (NASDAQ: FB)

Price at time of writing: $183.20 USD

Founded in 2004 in Cambridge MA by four Harvard Students and currently residing in Silicon Valley, CA, Facebook provides the largest social media platform in the world with 40 billion active users. It also provides one of the largest advertising and marketing platforms in the world between FB and its acquisition of Instagram.

Current sales stand at $56 billion per year and climbing as the premier provider of these services to major companies, individuals and government entities. Its recently released balance sheets show consistent growth, indicating that it has a strong business model.

It maintains low risk with very little competition in the area and is poised for a bright future in the industry. Its strong relationship with many large companies and its cutting edge research to improve its platform is key to keeping it strong.

The fact it is an industry leader will keep this a stable stock for most investors and it has the potential to go as high as the tech sector.

JD.com (NASDAQ: JD)

Price at time of writing: $29.50 USD

Founded in 1998 and currently residing in Beijing China, JD.com is a provider of e-commerce and consumer products in China and the Far East.

Current sales stand at $65 billion per year and climbing as the premier provider of these services to the areas around China.

It maintains low risk with very little competition in the area and is poised for a bright future in the industry. Its strong relationships with many local governments and its cutting edge research to improve its operations are key to keeping it strong.

The fact it is an industry leader will keep this a stable stock for some investors (that are not bothered by the volatility of China) and it has the potential to go as high as the tech sector.

Shake Shack (NASDAQ: SHAK)

Price at time of writing: $61.25 USD

Founded in 2004 and currently residing in New York, NY, Shake Shack is a provider of fast-casual food and shakes in a clean and inexpensive environment. It started as a simple hot dog cart and has grown to a chain with 200 locations in both the US and foreign countries.

Current sales stand at $650 million per year and climbing as a premier provider of American style food in a quick clean environment. They are a few steps above typical fast food and have better service and ingredients. Think Chipotle for American style food.

It maintains low risk with very little competition in the area of fast casual burgers/shakes and is poised for a bright future in the industry. Its strong reputation and fast expansion within the niche system is key to keeping it strong.

The fact it is an industry leader will keep this a stable stock for most investors and it has the potential to go as high as the

Everyman Investing

food sector.

Tesla (NASDAQ: TSLA)

Price at time of writing: $263.33 USD

Founded in 2003 and currently residing in Palo Alto, CA, Tesla is the premier provider of renewable energy and electric cars to the USA and the world. In fact, they have done so well that when one thinks of an electric car, they think Tesla.

Current sales stand at $21.4 billion per year and climbing as the premier provider of these services to major companies, individuals, and government entities.

It maintains low risk with very little competition in the area and is poised for a bright future in the industry. Its strong relationship with many large companies and its cutting edge research to improve its products is key to keeping it strong.

The fact it is an industry leader will keep this a stable stock for most investors and it has the potential to go as high as the tech sector.

Nike (NASDAQ: NKE)

Price at time of writing: $88.50 USD

Founded in 1964 and currently residing in Beaverton, OR, Nike is a provider of athletic equipment, apparel, and shoes for individuals, teams, and companies. One of the largest in the niche with exclusive contracts with many of the professional, high school, and college sports teams and leagues. Its revenues continue to climb year after year as evident in their recently released financial statements, which can be found on their website.

Current sales stand at $36 billion per year and climbing as the premier provider of these services and products.

It maintains low risk with very little competition in the area and is poised for a bright future in the industry. Its strong relationship with many large companies, sports leagues, and colleges and its cutting edge research to improve products will keep it strong.

The fact it is an industry leader will keep this a stable stock for most investors and it has the potential to go as high as the sports sector.

Boeing (NASDAQ: BA)

Price at time of writing: $376.76 USD

Founded in 1916 in Seattle, WA and currently residing in Chicago, IL, Boeing is a provider of aircraft, weapons, and military equipment for the US government, Allies, and airlines. In addition to providing the Boeing Jet Series, it also has exclusive duties with many government entities for year 2018/2019.

Current sales stand at $102 billion per year and climbing as the premier provider of these services to major companies and government entities. It has contracts with both the USA and its Allies for military equipment.

It maintains low risk with very little competition in the area and is poised for a bright future in the industry. Its strong relationships with the government and large companies and its cutting edge research to improve its products are key to keeping it strong.

The fact that it is an industry leader will keep this a stable stock for most investors and it has the potential to go as high as the tech sector.

Visa (NASDAQ: V)

Price at time of writing: $161.68 USD

Founded in 1958 and currently residing in Foster City, CA, Visa is the number one provider of branded credit, debit, and prepaid charge cards in the world. In addition, it provides payment processing and financial support to many banks and financial institutions.

Current sales stand at $18 billion per year and climbing as the premier provider of these services to major banks, companies, and government entities.

It maintains low risk with very little competition in the area and is poised for a bright future in the industry. Its strong relationship with many large companies and its cutting edge research to improve its communication system is key to keeping it strong.

The fact it is an industry leader will keep this a stable stock for most investors and it has the potential to go as high as the tech and finance sector.

Nokia (NASDAQ: NOK)

Price at time of writing: $5.83 USD

Founded in 1865 and near Helsinki, Finland as a pulp mill, Nokia is currently a provider of web-based communication, wireless communication devices, smart devices, and sell their support system to businesses, schools, and individuals.

Current sales stand at $22.5 billion per year and climbing as one of the premier providers of these services to major companies, individuals, and government entities.

It maintains average risk despite the competition in the area and is poised for a bright future in the industry. Its strong relationship with many large companies and its cutting edge research to improve its communication system is key to keeping it strong.

The fact it is an industry leader will keep this a stable stock for most investors and it has the potential to go as high as the tech sector.

Skyworks Solutions (NASDAQ: SWKS)

Price at time of writing: $89.73 USD

Founded in 2002 and currently residing in Woburn, MA, Skyworks Solutions is a provider of semiconductors, sound adapters, and wireless networking systems for wireless infrastructure.

Current sales stand at $3.2 million per year and climbing as a rising provider of these services to major companies and government entities.

It maintains average risk with the limited competition in the area and is poised for a bright future in the industry. Its strong relationship with many large companies and its cutting edge research to improve its communication system is key to keeping it strong.

The fact it is an industry leader will keep this a stable stock for most investors and it has the potential to go as high as the tech sector.

Samsung (NASDAQ: SSNLF)

Price at time of writing: $44.20 USD

Founded in 1937 and currently residing in Seoul, South Korea, Samsung is a provider of wireless communication devices, smart technology, and is a leader in the research around it.

Current sales stand at $210 billion per year and climbing as the premier provider of these services to major companies and government entities. It stands as the number one provider of wireless equipment, even taking a leading position above Apple.

It maintains low risk even with some prime competition in the sector and is poised for a bright future in the industry. Its strong relationship with many large companies and its cutting edge research to improve its communication system is key to keeping it strong. Also, Samsung has become the go-to company for manufacturers using android based systems and products and will continue to grow within that niche.

The fact it is an industry leader will keep this a stable stock for most investors and it has the potential to go as high as the tech sector.

United Technologies (NASDAQ: UTX)

Price at time of writing: $139.14 USD

Founded in 1934 and currently residing in Farmington, CE, United Technologies is a provider of engines, HVAC components, security systems, elevators/escalators, and other industrial products. It has many subsidiaries, a few of them are shown below as listed on their website.

- Otis Elevator Company: Manufacturer, installer, and servicer of elevators, escalators, and moving walkways.

- Pratt & Whitney: Designs and builds aircraft engines and gas turbines.

- Collins Aerospace: Designs and manufactures aerospace systems for commercial, regional, corporate and military aircraft.

- UTC Climate, Controls & Security: Makes fire detection and suppression systems, access control systems. Conditioning, and refrigeration systems.

- United Technologies Research Center (UTRC): A centralized research facility.

Current sales stand at $66 billion per year and climbing as the premier provider of these services to major companies and government entities. Earnings reports show strong growth, indicating that it is a major player with a successful business model.

It maintains low risk with very little competition in the area and is poised for a bright future in the industry. Its strong relationship with many large companies and its cutting edge research to improve its communication system is key to keeping it strong.

The fact it is an industry leader will keep this a stable stock for most investors and it has the potential to go as high as the logistics sector.

Clorox (NASDAQ: CLX)

Price at time of writing: $153.39 USD

Founded in 1916 and currently residing in Oakland, CA, Clorox is a provider of both chemicals, consumer products, and food products for consumers. It operates under several well-known brands like Burt's Bees and many others.

Current sales stand at $6.1 billion per year and climbing as the premier provider of these products to consumers.

It maintains low risk with very little competition in the area and is poised for a bright future in the industry. Its strong relationships with many large companies and consumer brand loyalty indicate that it will remain a strong player.

Everyman Investing

The fact it is an industry leader will keep this a stable stock for most investors and it has the potential to go as high as the retail sector.

Duke Energy (NASDAQ: DUK)

Price at time of writing: $89.42 USD

Founded in 1904 and currently residing in Charlotte, NC, Duke Energy is a provider of energy and utilities to many customers across the USA, Canada, and South America. Duke Energy now has many subsidiaries, both in the USA and internationally.

Current sales stand at $22 billion per year and climbing as the premier provider of these services to major utilities and government entities. It operates 10% of the major utilities in the USA.

It maintains low risk with very little competition in the area and is poised for a bright future in the industry. Its strong relationship with many large companies is key to keeping it strong.

The fact it is an industry leader will keep this a stable stock for most investors and it has the potential to go as high as the biotech and utilities sectors.

Chapter Six Growth Stocks Part 3

Realty Income (NASDAQ: O)

Price at time of writing: $69.96 USD

Founded in 1950 and currently residing in San Diego, CA, Realty Income was originally a real estate management company but now is a REIT. This, as you remember from earlier chapters, pools money for investment in real estate and pays dividends based on the profits. This is a rare thing as it is both growth and income stock.

Current sales stand at $1.25 billion per year and climbing as the premier provider of investment in commercial and industrial properties.

It maintains low risk with very little competition in the area and is poised for a bright future in the industry. Its strong relationship with many large companies and the ability to buy larger properties will keep it ahead of the game.

The fact it is an industry leader will keep this a stable stock for most investors and it has the potential to go as high as the real estate sector. Even in a downturn, it will remain stable.

3M (NASDAQ: MMM)

Price at time of writing: $218.52 USD

Everyman Investing

Founded in 1902 and currently residing in Maplewood, MN, 3M was originally a mining company but now has a huge stake in the consumer product manufacturing, healthcare, security, and marketing sectors.

Current sales stand at $31 billion per year and climbing as the premier provider of these services to individuals. They also have a significant degree of brand loyalty in their manufactured brands. With a strong recent income report published to their website, 3M is set to remain successful.

It maintains low risk with its diversified businesses. Its strong relationship with many large companies and its consumer brand loyalty and reputation will keep it strong.

The fact it is an industry leader will keep this a stable stock for most investors and it has the potential to go as high as the many sectors it works in.

Starbucks (NASDAQ: SBUX)

Price at time of writing: $75.35 USD

Founded in 1971 and currently residing in Seattle, WA, Starbucks is a provider of coffee and cafe items across thousands of locations nationwide and internationally.

Current sales stand at $23 billion per year and climbing as the premier provider of these products to the public through

20,000 stores in 62 countries around the world, and growing.

It maintains low risk even with the competition in the area and is poised for a bright future in the industry. Its strong relationship with many large companies and its cutting edge research to improve its communication system are key to keeping it strong.

The fact it is an industry leader will keep this a stable stock for most investors.

Abbvie (NASDAQ: ABBV)

Price at time of writing: $78.63 USD

Founded in 2013 and currently residing in near Chicago, IL, Abbvie is a provider of cancer drugs and research and is a spinoff of Abbott Labs.

Current sales stand at $32 billion per year and climbing as the premier provider of these drugs.

It maintains low risk with very little competition in the area and is poised for a bright future in the industry. Its strong relationship with many large companies and its cutting edge research to improve current drugs develop new ones is a boon.

The fact it is an industry leader will keep this a stable stock

Everyman Investing

for most investors.

TD Bank (NASDAQ: TD)

Price at time of writing: $55.61 USD

Founded in 1965 and currently residing in Toronto, Canada, TD Bank is Canada's largest bank and financial institution.

Current sales stand at $36 billion per year and climbing as the premier provider of these services to major companies and government entities.

It maintains low risk with very little competition in the area and is poised for a bright future in the industry. Its strong relationship with many large companies and its cutting edge research to improve its communication system is key to keeping it strong.

The fact it is an industry leader will keep this a stable stock for most investors.

Altria (NASDAQ: MO)

Price at time of writing: $54.58 USD

Founded in 1985 and currently residing in Henrico County, VA, Altria is a rebranding of the tobacco company Philip

Morris.

Current sales stand at $27 billion per year and climbing as the company revamps to stop the damage of the no-smoking campaign. It is venturing into the e-cig market and exploring areas such as cannabis.

It maintains average risk with very little competition in the area and but is the riskiest of the growth stocks as it must overcome its past. Its strong relationship with many large companies and its cutting edge research to improve and expand its offerings will keep it stable in the future.

The fact it is an industry leader will keep this a stable stock for most investors but due to past industry shifts, it should be watched closely.

International Paper (NASDAQ: IP)

Price at time of writing: $44.63 USD

Founded in 1898 in New York by a merging of 17 paper mills and currently residing in Memphis, TN, International Paper is a provider of paper and paper products to the US government and other governments as well as private companies.

Current sales stand at $21 billion per year and climbing as the premier provider of these services to major companies and government entities. It restructured in 2006 to become much leaner and offset the paperless revolution. It is researching other potentially useful materials like hemp and other alternatives to paper.

It maintains low risk with very little competition in the area and is poised for a bright future in the industry. Its strong relationship with many large companies and its cutting edge research to improve and diversify its products is a pro.

The fact it is an industry leader will keep this a stable stock for most investors. However, it is in a shrinking industry so keep your eye on this one.

Cisco (NASDAQ: CSCO)

Price at time of writing: $56.85 USD

Founded in 1985 and currently residing in San Francisco, CA, Cisco is a provider of web-based services and hardware/software, as well as infrastructure components to enable the use of Wi-Fi and net technologies.

Current sales stand at $46 billion per year and climbing as the premier provider of these services to major companies and government entities. Its growth is demonstrated by its past year's income available on their website.

It maintains low risk with very little competition in the area and is poised for a bright future in the industry. Its strong relationship with many large companies and its cutting edge research to improve its communication system are key to keeping it strong.

The fact it is an industry leader will keep this a stable stock for most investors.

CVS (NASDAQ: CVS)

Price at time of writing: $52.96 USD

Founded in 1996 and currently residing in Woonsocket, RI, CVS is a provider of medical research and pharmacy services to businesses, medical professionals, and individuals

Current sales stand at $184 billion per year and climbing as the premier provider of these services to major companies and the general public. It has consistently grown and has expanded into health clinics and insurance.

It maintains low risk with limited competition in the area and is poised for a bright future in the industry. Its strong relationship with many large companies and its cutting edge research to improve its offerings is key to keeping it strong.

The fact it is an industry leader will keep this a stable stock for most investors.

Walgreens (NASDAQ: WBA)

Price at time of writing: $53.52 USD

Founded in 1901 and currently residing in Chicago, IL, Walgreens is a provider of medical research and pharmacy services to businesses, medical professionals, and individuals

Current sales stand at $183 billion per year and climbing as the premier provider of these services to major companies and government entities as well as the general public.

It maintains low risk with limited competition in the area and is poised for a bright future in the industry. Its strong relationship with many large companies and its cutting edge research to improve its offerings are key to keeping it strong.

The fact it is an industry leader will keep this a stable stock for most investors.

Molson Coors (NASDAQ: TAP)

Price at time of writing: $63.87 USD

Founded in 2005 via a merger between Molson of Canada and Coors Co. and currently residing in Denver, CO, it is a major provider of beer and other alcoholic beverages/consumer products worldwide.

Current sales stand at $4.8 billion per year and climbing as the premier provider of these services to major companies and government entities.

It maintains average risk despite the competition in the sector and is poised for a bright future in the industry. Its strong relationship with many large wholesalers and its cutting brand loyalty and reputation for value will keep it strong.

The fact it is an industry leader will keep this a stable stock for most investors and since beer is usually stable during downturns you don't need to fear a recession.

NXP Semiconductors (NASDAQ: NXPI)

Price at time of writing: $100.49 USD

Founded in 1953 and currently residing in the Netherlands, NXP Semiconductors is a provider of semiconductors and infrastructure components for the wireless industry.

Current sales stand at $9 billion per year and climbing as a premier provider of these services to major companies and government entities around the world.

It maintains low risk with very little competition in the area and is poised for a bright future in the industry. Its strong relationships with many large companies and its cutting edge research to improve its communication system are key to keeping it strong. In addition, it has one of the best supply and distribution chains in the world including China, Thailand, Japan, Europe, and the USA.

The fact it is an industry leader will keep this a stable stock for most investors.

Viacom (NASDAQ: VIA)

Price at time of writing: $36.66 USD

Founded in 2013 and currently residing in NY, NY, Viacom is a worldwide entertainment provider. It was formed by a merger and consolidation between CBS and other media companies.

Current sales stand at $12.5 billion per year and climbing as the premier provider of these services to the world. Its holdings have a foothold in TV and movies and include well-known names such as Paramount and Nickelodeon.

It maintains average risk despite the competition in the area and is poised for a bright future in the industry. Its strong relationship with many large companies and its cutting edge research to improve its communication system are key to keeping it strong.

The fact it is an industry leader will keep this a stable stock for most investors.

Kraft Heinz (NASDAQ: KHC)

Price at time of writing: $32.70 USD

Founded in 2015 and currently residing in Pittsburg, PA and Chicago, IL, the company is a merger of the companies Kraft and Heinz. It is a provider of consumer products and foods.

Current sales stand at $6.5 billion per year and climbing as the premier provider of these products with unrivaled brand loyalty. Its recently published sales chart can be accessed from its website and shows consistent growth each year.

It maintains low risk with very little competition in the area and is poised for a bright future in the industry. Its strong relationship with many large companies and its ever-expanding brand list keeps it an industry leader.

The fact it is an industry leader will keep this a stable stock for most investors.

Tencent (NASDAQ: TCTZF)

Price at time of writing: $49.76 USD

Founded in 1998 and currently residing in China, Tencent is a conglomerate that produces a wide range of technology including AI, wireless products, telecommunications, and consumer products. Some of its well-known products are video games, online payments (Paipal), e-commerce, and the search engine Soso. In addition, they are a Google AdSense partner and run their own social media platform known as TencentQ.

Current sales stand at $300 billion per year and climbing as the premier provider of these services to major companies and Far East government entities.

It maintains low risk with very little competition in the area and is poised for a bright future in the industry. Its strong relationship with many large companies and its cutting edge research to improve its communication system are key to keeping it strong.

Huya (NASDAQ: HUYA)

Price at time of writing: $22.72 USD

Founded in 2008 and currently residing in San Francisco, CA, Huya is a provider of web-based communication to businesses and allows the use of its APIs to perform a variety of communications like texts/calls via their databases.

Current sales stand at $650 million per year and climbing as the premier provider of these services to major companies and government entities.

It maintains low risk with very little competition in the area and is poised for a bright future in the industry. Its strong relationship with many large companies and its cutting edge research to improve its communication system are key to keeping it strong.

Weibo (NASDAQ: WB)

Price at time of writing: $70.40 USD

Founded in 2008 and currently residing in San Francisco, CA, Weibo is a provider of web-based communication to businesses and allows the use of its APIs to enable a variety of communications like texts/calls via their databases.

Current sales stand at $650 million per year and climbing as the premier provider of these services to major companies and government entities.

It maintains low risk with very little competition in the area and is poised for a bright future in the industry. Its strong relationship with many large companies and its cutting edge research to improve its communication system are key to keeping it strong.

It is a good investment for anyone not scared of investment in China.

Everyman Investing

China Mobile (NASDAQ: CHL)

Price at time of writing: $47.14 USD

Founded in 1997 and currently residing in Hong Kong, China Mobile is a provider of wireless communications and wireless products. It is semi owned by the Chinese Government and enjoys a great deal of protections that others do not have.

Current sales stand at $16 billion per year and climbing as the premier provider of these services to major companies and government entities.

It maintains low risk with very little competition in the area and with the protection of the Chinese government, it is quickly expanding into rural areas of the country with unprecedented ability to cut consumer costs. Its strong relationship with many large companies and its cutting edge research to improve its communication system are key to keeping it strong.

It is a good investment for those not worried about potential fluctuations in the Chinese market.

Aurora Cannabis (NASDAQ: ACB)

Price at time of writing: $9.14 USD

Founded in 2013 and currently residing in Edmonton AB,

Canada, Aurora Cannabis is a provider of marijuana and related products.

Current sales stand at $18 million per year and climbing as a premier provider of these services to all areas where marijuana is legal (and probably some that are not).

It maintains low risk with very little competition in the area and is poised for a bright future in the industry.

It is a good investment for anyone not scared of investment in cannabis or foreign businesses.

Aphria (NASDAQ: APHA)

Price at time of writing: $7.87 USD

Founded in 2014 and currently residing in Toronto, Canada, Aphria is a provider of marijuana and related products, mostly to the medical industry.

Current sales stand at $36 million per year and climbing as a premier provider of these services to all areas in the medical arena, which provides a much bigger market than some of its competitors that rely on the recreational market alone.

It maintains low risk with very little competition in the area and is poised for a bright future in the industry.

It is a good investment for anyone not scared of investment in

Everyman Investing

cannabis or foreign businesses.

Tilray (NASDAQ: TLRY)

Price at time of writing: $51.24 USD

Founded in 2014 and currently residing in Narimo BC, Canada, Tilray is a provider of marijuana and related products.

Current sales stand at $30 million per year and climbing as a premier provider of these services, with distribution and branches in Germany, South America, Australia, and New Zealand. This provides a much bigger market than some of its competitors that rely on the North American market.

It maintains low risk with very little competition in the area and is poised for a bright future in the industry.

It is a good investment for anyone not scared of investment in cannabis or foreign businesses.

Intel (NASDAQ: INTC)

Price at time of writing: $58.82 USD

Founded in 1968 and currently residing in Santa Clara, CA, Intel is the number two (2nd only to Samsung) provider of semiconductors and wireless communications infrastructure and product components.

Current sales stand at $70 billion per year and climbing as a major provider of these services to large companies and government entities.

It maintains low risk with very little competition in the area and is poised for a bright future in the industry. Its strong relationship with many large companies and its cutting edge research to improve its communication system are key to keeping it strong.

It is a great investment for any investor!

Corning (NASDAQ: GLW)

Price at time of writing: $34.46 USD

Founded in 1852 and currently residing in Corning, NY, Corning is a provider of glass, ceramic, and wireless optics.

Current sales stand at $11 billion per year and climbing as the premier provider of these services to major companies and government entities.

It maintains low risk with very little competition in the area and is poised for a bright future in the industry. Its strong relationship with many large companies and its cutting edge research to improve its communication system are key to keeping it strong.

It is a great investment for any investor.

Comcast (NASDAQ: CMCSA)

Price at time of writing: $41.88 USD

Founded in 1953 and currently residing in Philadelphia, PA, Comcast is a provider of broadcasting, telecommunications, and streaming technologies. It is the result of a merger of several companies including NBC, Comcast, and a division of Verizon. Some of its holdings are cable powerhouses such as Syfy and Bravo, as well as the streaming giant HULU.

Current sales stand at $94 billion per year and climbing as the premier provider of these services to major companies and government entities. Its revenue has grown year after year, as shown in the recent sales chart on their website.

It maintains low risk with very little competition in the area and is poised for a bright future in the industry. Its strong relationship with many large companies and its cutting edge research to improve its communication system are key to keeping it strong.

Dell (NASDAQ: DELL)

Price at time of writing: $66.02 USD

Founded in 1984 and currently residing in Round Rock, TX, Dell is a provider of computers, parts, and wireless devices. It has made a name for itself with new innovations in logistics and supply chain operation.

Current sales stand at $78 billion per year and climbing as a premier provider of these products to individuals, major companies, and government entities.

It maintains average risk with the competition in the area and is poised for a bright future in the industry. Its strong relationship with many large companies, brand loyalty, and its cutting edge research to improve its products are a huge pro.

Chapter Seven Growth Stocks Part 4

Cloudera (NASDAQ: CLDR)

Price at time of writing: $10.91 USD

Founded in 2002 and currently residing in Palo Alto, CA, Cloudera is a provider of a software platform for data engineering, data warehousing, machine learning and analytics that runs in the cloud or on premises. Basically, it is a cloud computing repository provider.

Current sales stand at $650 million per year and climbing as a premier provider of these services to major companies and government entities.

It maintains low risk with very little competition in the area and is poised for a bright future in the industry. Its strong relationship with many large companies and its cutting edge research to improve its infrastructure are key to keeping it strong.

It is a strong investment for any investor of any level.

Equinix (NASDAQ: EQIX)

Price at time of writing: $452.50 USD

Founded in 1998 and currently residing in Redwood, CA, Equinix is a provider of internet connection and data centers.

Current sales stand at $4.5 billion per year and climbing as a rising provider of these services to major companies and government entities.

It is average to low risk with some competition in the area and is poised for a bright future in the industry. Its strong relationship with many large companies and its cutting edge research to improve its infrastructure are key to keeping it strong.

It is a very strong stock for those that can afford the purchase price.

FireEye (NASDAQ: FEYE)

Price at time of writing: $15.83 USD

Founded in 2004 and currently residing in Mittapis, CA, FireEye is a provider of cybersecurity and antivirus protection systems.

Current sales stand at $880 million per year and climbing as the premier provider of these services to major companies and government entities.

It maintains low risk with very little competition in the area and is poised for a bright future in the industry. Its strong relationship with many large companies and its cutting edge research to improve its communication system are key to

Everyman Investing

keeping it strong.

It is a very strong stock for any investor at a very affordable price.

Intuit (NASDAQ: INTU)

Price at time of writing: $264.87 USD

Founded in 1983 and currently residing in Mountain View, CA, Intuit is a provider of web-based accounting, tax preparation, and bookkeeping under the brands TurboTax, Quickbooks, Mintm, and Proconnect.

Current sales stand at $5 billion per year and climbing as the premier provider of these services to individuals, major companies, and government entities. Its recent history of income was published on its website and shows consistent growth over time.

It maintains low risk with very little competition in the area and is poised for a bright future in the industry. Its strong relationship with many large companies and its cutting edge research to improve its delivery and pricing are key to keeping it strong.

Veeva Systems (NASDAQ: VEEV)

Price at time of writing: $137.37 USD

Founded in 2007 and currently residing in Pleasanton, CA, Veeva Systems is a provider of cloud-based and content management services.

Current sales stand at $65 billion per year and climbing as the premier provider of these services to major companies and government entities.

It maintains low risk despite competition in the area and is poised for a bright future in the industry. Its strong relationship with many large companies and its cutting edge research to improve its platforms are key to keeping it strong.

It is a strong stock for any investor.

Trade Desk (NASDAQ: TTD)

Price at time of writing: $208.27 USD

Founded in 2009 and currently residing in Ventura, CA, Trade Desk is a provider of web-based investing and brokerage services. It is one of the leaders in the direct investment sector that allows for instant purchases across several exchanges.

Current sales stand at $477 million per year and climbing as the premier provider of these services worldwide. Its recent financials as published on their investor relations page have shown excellent growth, indicating a strong position in the industry.

It maintains a low risk with very little new competition in the area and is poised for a bright future in the industry. Its strong relationships with the exchanges/customers and its cutting edge research to improve its communication system are key to keeping it strong.

Altogether this makes it a great stock for any investor.

Iron Mountain (NASDAQ: IRM)

Price at time of writing: $35.84 USD

Founded in 1951 and currently residing in Boston, MA, Iron Mountain is a provider of web-based and software-based enterprise information and data management.

Current sales stand at $3.5 billion per year and climbing as the premier provider of these services to major companies and government entities.

It maintains low risk with very little competition in the area and is poised for a bright future in the industry. Its strong relationship with many large companies and its cutting edge research to improve its communication system are key to keeping it strong.

It is a good stock for any level of investor.

IBM (NASDAQ: IBM)

Price at time of writing: $140.05 USD

Founded in 1911 and currently residing in Armont, NY, IBM initially started as a provider of office machines and later computers. Today it provides a plethora of computers, software, components, and wireless products to businesses, government, and individuals. It makes up one of the core companies of the DOW Jones Average.

Current sales stand at $79 billion per year and climbing as the premier provider of these services to major companies and government entities. IBM has battled back from recession losses to be sitting as a stable stock. The published earnings report on the IBM website shows excellent stability and growth in recent years.

It maintains low risk despite the competition in the area and is poised for a bright future in the industry. Its strong relationship with many large companies and its cutting edge research to improve its communication system are key to keeping it strong.

A very stable stock for any level of investor.

Taiwan Semiconductor (NASDAQ: TSM)

Everyman Investing

Price at time of writing: $45.41 USD

Founded in 1987 and currently residing in Taiwan, Taiwan Semiconductor is a provider of semiconductors and wireless infrastructure components.

Current sales stand at $15 billion per year and climbing as an on the rise provider of these products to major companies and government entities.

It maintains low risk despite the competition in the area and is poised for a bright future in the industry especially in the emerging Far East market. Its strong relationship with many large companies and its cutting edge research to improve its products will keep it strong.

A good investment for any investor not afraid of the emerging world.

Thermo Fisher Scientific (NASDAQ: TMO)

Price at time of writing: $263.95 USD

Founded in 2006 and currently residing in San Francisco, CA, Thermo Fisher Scientific resulted from a merger of Thermo Electron and Fisher Scientific. It is a provider of genetic research and micro-precision lab and medical equipment. It owns and supplies under many different brands including Thermo Scientific, Applied Biosystems, and Invitrogen.

Current sales stand at $20 billion per year and climbing as the premier provider of these services to major companies and government entities.

It maintains low risk with very little competition in the area and is poised for a bright future in the industry. Its strong relationship with many large companies and its cutting edge research to improve its systems are key to keeping it strong.

A wise investment for any level of investor.

Exact Sciences (NASDAQ: EXAS)

Price at time of writing: $95.46 USD

Founded in 1995 and currently residing in Madison, WI, Exact Sciences is a lab that concentrates on genetic and microbial research for the purpose of mapping risk down to the atom. It has an exclusive relationship with FDA and conducts a lot of trials for them.

Current sales stand at $6 billion per year and climbing as the premier provider of these services to major companies and government entities.

It maintains low risk with very little competition in the area and is poised for a bright future in the industry. Its strong relationship with many large companies and its cutting edge research to improve its communication system are key to

Everyman Investing

keeping it strong.

A very economical and wise choice for any investor.

Myriad Genetics (NASDAQ: MYGN)

Price at time of writing: $32.24 USD

Founded in 1991 and currently residing in Salt Lake City, UT, Myriad Genetics is a provider of multiple types of genetic testing and other diagnostic products based on molecular biology. Its flagship product is Prolaris, which can map the risk of colon cancer and has extended the lives of many patients.

Current sales stand at $26 billion per year and climbing as the premier provider of these services to major companies and government entities.

It maintains low risk with very little competition in the area and is poised for a bright future in the industry. Its strong relationship with many large companies and its cutting edge research to improve its communication system are key to keeping it strong.

A very economical and wise choice for any investor.

NeoGenomics (NASDAQ: NEO)

Price at time of writing: $19.88 USD

Founded in 2002 and currently residing in Fort Myers, FL, NeoGenomics is a lab that concentrates on genetic and microbial research for the purpose of treating cancer.

Current sales stand at $10 billion per year and climbing as the premier provider of these services to major companies and government entities.

It maintains low risk with very little competition in the area and is poised for a bright future in the industry. Its strong relationship with many large companies and its cutting edge research to improve its communication system are key to keeping it strong.

A very economical and wise choice for any investor.

Nvidia (NASDAQ: NVDA)

Price at time of writing: $191.88 USD

Founded in 1992 and currently residing in Santa Clara, CA, Nvidia is a provider of platforms for gaming, data centers, auto, pro visualization, and now AI. It has garnered a following for its gaming CPUs. Per its website, it does business with the brands GeForce, Quadro, Tegra, and Tesla.

Current sales stand at $9 billion per year and climbing as the premier provider of these services to major companies and government entities.

It maintains low risk with very little competition in the area and is poised for a bright future in the industry. Its strong relationship with many large companies and its cutting edge research to improve its products are key to keeping it strong.

It is a very wise stock for any level of investor.

Micron Technology (NASDAQ: MU)

Price at time of writing: $43.20 USD

Founded in 1978 and currently residing in Boise, ID, Micron Technology is holding and parent company to many subsidiaries that produce computers and semiconductors, and wireless products.

Current sales stand at $20 billion per year and climbing as the premier provider of these services to major companies and government entities.

It maintains low risk with very little competition in the area and is poised for a bright future in the industry. Its strong relationship with many large companies and its cutting edge research to improve its technology system are key to keeping it strong.

Ross (NASDAQ: ROST)

Price at time of writing: $98.65 USD

Founded in 1982 and currently residing in Dublin, CA, Ross is a provider of name brand clothing for men, women, and children and consumer products in a secondary setting. It buys closeouts and overstocks and resells them at over 1000 stores across the Midwest and Northeast.

Current sales stand at $12 billion per year and climbing as the premier provider of these products at low prices. This type of store remains stable in a recession as discounting is big.

It maintains low risk with very little competition in the area and is poised for a bright future in the industry. Its great relationship with retailers and brand awareness is keeping it strong.

A recession proof stock which should hold strong in the coming 36 months.

Amgen (NASDAQ: AMGN)

Price at time of writing: $179.20 USD

Founded in 1980 and currently residing in Thousand Oaks, CA, Amgen works in the pharma industry related to preventing infection in chemotherapy patients and blocking betta transmitters in cancer cells.

Current sales stand at $23 billion per year and climbing as the premier provider of these services to medical providers and

Everyman Investing

researchers.

It maintains low risk with very little competition in the area and is poised for a bright future in the industry. Its strong relationship with many large companies and its cutting edge research to improve its products is key to keeping it strong.

A high potential stock for any investor level.

Dollar Tree (NASDAQ: DLTR)

Price at time of writing: $109.85 USD

Founded in 1986 and currently residing in Norfolk, VA, Dollar Tree is a retailer of low-cost items, food, and consumer products under the Names Dollar Tree and Family Dollar across North America.

Current sales stand at $22 billion per year and climbing as the premier provider of discount items.

It maintains low risk with very little competition in the area and is poised for a bright future in the industry. Its strong relationship with many large companies and its cutting its many locations make it a primary stock and poised for success.

Like Ross, a good solid recession-proof stock for any investor.

Concho Resources (NASDAQ: CXO)

Price at time of writing: $128.31 USD

Founded in 2004 and currently residing in Midland, TX, Concho Resources is a provider of research into bio-carbon and alternative energies. Its vast petroleum holdings make it very successful.

Current sales stand at $4 billion per year and climbing as the premier provider of these services to major companies and government entities.

It maintains low risk with very little competition in the area and is poised for a bright future in the industry. Its strong relationship with many large companies and its cutting edge research to improve its energy offerings/green energy in general are key to keeping it strong.

Great for any investor, especially those interested in green energy.

Nutanix (NASDAQ: NTNX)

Price at time of writing: $43.02 USD

Founded in 2009 and currently residing in India, Nutanix is a provider of web-based cloud business solutions for hyper-converged infrastructure (HCI) appliances and software-defined storage.

Everyman Investing

Current sales stand at $700 million per year and climbing as the premier provider of these services to major companies and government entities in the Far and Middle East.

It maintains low risk with very little competition in the area and is poised for a bright future in the industry. Its strong relationship with many large companies and its cutting edge research to improve its communication system are key to keeping it strong.

A good investment for those not afraid of investing in the Middle East.

Dropbox (NASDAQ: DBX)

Price at time of writing: $23.42 USD

Founded in 2007 and currently residing in San Francisco, CA, Dropbox is a provider of online file sharing platforms in 17 languages that allow syncing and easy sharing of projects with people all over the world. It offers several levels of service each with different abilities and functions.

Current sales stand at $20 billion per year and climbing as the premier provider of these services to individuals, colleges/schools major companies and government entities.

It maintains low risk with very little competition in the area and is poised for a bright future in the industry. Its strong relationship with many large companies and its cutting edge research to improve its communication system are key to keeping it strong.

Competition from Google will be tough, but the market is big enough for both to co-exist.

Boingo Wireless (NASDAQ: WIFI)

Price at time of writing: $23.68 USD

Founded in 2001 and currently residing in Los Angeles, CA, Boingo Wireless is a provider of wireless internet service to enabled devices with over 1,000,000 wireless networks to use. It is an alternative to the major carriers and data services. It operates and sells a variety of products/services such as traditional wireless and broadband.

Current sales stand at $250 million per year and climbing as the premier provider of these services to major companies and government entities. Including various airports and transportation hubs.

It maintains low risk with very little competition in the area and is poised for a bright future in the industry. Its strong relationship with many large companies and its cutting edge research to improve its communication system are key to keeping it strong.

Genius Brands International (NASDAQ: GNUS)

Price at time of writing: $2.00 USD

Founded in 2013 and currently residing in Los Angeles, CA, Genius Brands International is an entertainment and animation company (formerly DIC) that formed as the result of multiple mergers. It is rebuilding its business and venturing into CGI. This is definitely a company to watch for the future.

Current sales stand at $300 million per year and climbing as it will be a premiere animation company going forward.

It maintains low risk despite the competition in the area due to its strong branding and its past favorites such as Inspector Gadget and Dennis the Menace.

With a industry-wide trend towards tried and true franchises, Genius Brands is poised to be on the up and up over the next few years.

Eastman Kodak (NASDAQ: KODK)

Price at time of writing: $2.46 USD

Founded in 1888 and currently residing in Rochester, NY, Eastman Kodak is a provider of various graphics and art products, software, and devices. It was once the leader in film and photography and invented the digital camera. It has struggled to make a comeback but is poised to reenter the market with its new medical imaging products as well.

It maintains low risk despite the competition in the area and is poised for a bright future in the industry. Its strong relationship with many large companies and its cutting edge research to improve its products, as well as its brand recognition are key to keeping it strong.

This one could go either way, but the medical imaging market potential makes it a solid play for any investor that is willing to buy and hold for an extended time.

Arcimoto (NASDAQ: FUV)

Price at time of writing: $4.00 USD

Founded in 2007 and currently residing in Eugene, OR, Arcimoto is a provider of electric motorized transportation, including tandem two and three wheel bikes. Poised in an industry that is erupting as people move away from cars, Arcimoto is poised to be a leader.

Current sales stand at $650 million per year and climbing as the premier provider of these products to the public.

It maintains low risk with very little competition in the area and is poised for a bright future in the industry. As the industry of green transportation grows so will it.

A great and cheap option for those willing to buy and hold for many years.

Conclusion

Investing your money in the stock market (or anywhere else!) can be overwhelming, but it doesn't have to be.

I hope this information has been beneficial to you and has given you a foundation to invest some of the more unknown companies. There has never been a more exciting time for the market than right now. Even if you feel like you missed the boat with the Apples and Amazons of the world, don't worry, it's never too to get your piece of the pie.

Using dollar cost averaging and putting money into the market each month is a great way to invest. It helps make your investing automatic and allows you to smooth out your investments into a market that moves up and down in an unpredictable way.

Remember to do additional research outside of what you've learned in this book. And for your own sanity, don't check your investments on a daily basis.

Growth stocks in particular can be a volatile market, and you have to be willing to accept that if you are to make long term profits. Perhaps most importantly, don't panic sell if you see a dip in the market.

I wish you the best of luck in the cryptocurrency market, and I hope you make a lot of money.

Everyman Investing

Finally, if this book has proved useful to you, I'd appreciate it if you took 2 minutes to leave it a review on Amazon.

www.ingramcontent.com/pod-product-compliance
Lightning Source LLC
Chambersburg PA
CBHW060855170526
45158CB00001B/364